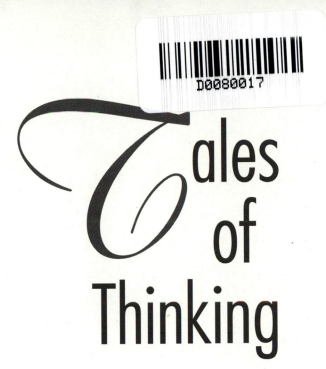

Tales of Thinking

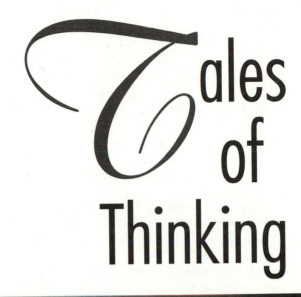

Tales of Thinking

Multiple Intelligences
in the Classroom

Paul Carreiro

Stenhouse Publishers
York, Maine

Stenhouse Publishers, 431 York Street, York, Maine 03909
www.stenhouse.com

Library of Congress Cataloging-in-Publication Data
Carreiro, Paul, 1957–
    Tales of thinking : multiple intelligences in the classroom / Paul Carreiro.
      p. cm.
    Includes bibliographical references and index.
    ISBN 1-57110-061-X (alk. paper)
    1. Learning.   2. Cognitive styles.   3. Intellect.   4. Teaching.
  I. Title.
  LB1060.C368   1997
    370.15′2—DC21
                                         97-25733
                                             CIP

Published simultaneously in Canada by
Pembroke Publishers Limited
538 Hood Road
Markham, Ontario L3R 3K9
ISBN 1-55138-090-0
Canadian Cataloging in Publication Data
Carreiro, Paul
  Tales of Thinking : multiple intelligences in the classroom
Includes bibliographical references and index.
ISBN 1-55138-090-0
1. Education, Elementary. I. Title.
LB1555.C37 1997 372 C97-93141-3

Cover and interior design by Ron Kosciak, *Dragonfly Design*
Typeset by Achorn Graphics

Manufactured in the United States of America on acid-free paper
02 01 00 99 98 97 9 8 7 6 5 4 3 2 1

for Elizabeth Rachel

Contents

Acknowledgments

The list of people who have helped to shape this book goes back many years and includes teachers in all parts of Canada. If you were one of those people, then I thank you. If you were kind enough to loan me work or tell a story from your class, then I thank you again.

Thanks are also due to the teachers and administrators in the City of York Board of Education for the support they have shown me over the years, and for being innovative enough to have the Teacher as Researcher program and an integrated child care/kindergarten model. Unlikely as it may be, I hope all of these organizations survive the next few years.

I would especially like to thank Agnes MacNeil, Ellen Farrelly, Sharon McMahon, Bev O'Brien, and Clare Keith for reading the various drafts and proposals. Thanks also to Karen Morrissey for all the gum she provided during the writing process. Special thanks to Philippa Stratton at Stenhouse for not panicking when she saw some of the more painful work-in-progress as well as for her critical feedback.

Two people deserve special mention. Laurel Whitham made innumerable critical comments on a key draft that consistently improved the work. Darcia Isenor asked questions that made me sit back and consider all the implications of the work and was instrumental in getting me to articulate what I really wanted to say in print. Darcia also played a critical role in doing reference checks and giving shape to some of the supporting material in the book.

I would also like to thank my teaching partner, Carol Hara, for her general support during the writing of this manuscript and for her persistence in making and remaking excellent programs for young children. Finally, and most of all, thanks to my wife, Agnes, for who she is and everything she does.

Part I

Beginning with
Multiple Intelligences

1

$\mathscr{B}$eginning Questions

She was—and probably still is—one of those larger-than-life children you sometimes have in a class. What I remember most is her hair, a gorgeous mass of black frizziness that could be transformed into almost any configuration. Larger-than-life hair for a larger-than-life child.

The hair sat on a round-cheeked four-year-old who was in constant motion.

Caroline danced up and down stairs, sang songs she had made up, and tried to stand on her head—all in the first two days of school. How many anecdotal notes can you have on one child after two days of school? I resolved to try to do a little more observing of the other children. At least it was a good thought.

On day three, while we were outside playing, she came to me and said, "When are we going to learn something in school?"

I replied in that clever, child-centered tone of voice, "I don't know. What would you like to learn?" This caught her off guard and allowed me to suggest that she think of what she'd like to know more about and then we'd talk. I actually felt pretty good with that response. I'd set a tone early in the year about my attitude toward teaching. I'd hoped to get her thinking about what she wanted to learn.

On day four, she came and repeated the question about when was she going to learn something and I repeated my question about what would she like to learn. She'd been thinking, not in any way I expected, of course, and said, "I don't know. You're the teacher."

Then she held up a penny and said, "This is a penny. When you teach me something, you get the penny. If you don't teach me something, no penny. You understand?"

And then she walked away.

*P*eople often ask me if I ever earned that penny. The answer is no, but it wasn't for lack of trying. The reality was that Caroline was learning. She was learning to think. Admittedly, she was learning to think more through what I *didn't* do than what I did.

More worrisome was the fact that she didn't know she was thinking, and I wondered how to show her. It is a real challenge to create an environment in which all children can think and at the same time to have children *know* they can think. Running a classroom where thinking is the main event helps children to do just this.

My conversation with Caroline took place in my junior/senior kindergarten class (four- and five-year-olds) in Toronto. I currently enjoy one of those ideal jobs I've been lucky enough to have a couple of times in my career. In the morning, I am a consultant to teachers who are trying to do their own reflective practice and action research, which means I get to hear teachers thinking in some wonderful ways. Their thinking challenges me to keep thinking about my own program. In the afternoon, I am a teacher in a regular community kindergarten, which means I get to hear young children thinking in wonderful ways. This, too, challenges me to extend my own learning. I share this position with Carol Hara, who is both my teaching and consulting partner. Many of the ideas and practices outlined in this book are the result of our joint planning. Better still, my school, Lambton Park Community School, has a childcare center in the same open space as the kindergarten, and there is an underlying assumption that the childcare and kindergarten staff should plan together, work together, and reflect together. Both childcare and kindergarten staff have adopted a multiple intelligence framework in planning programs for children and emphasize making smooth transitions between childcare and classroom.

I truly believe that thinking surrounds us all during the day, but that we only see it at moments. Sometimes it announces itself, as when Caroline told me what she was doing, but sometimes it is only clear when we look back over time. It has been twenty years since I began working with children and adults with physical and cognitive impairments. I have worked with all types of learners in all types of settings and in all types of roles. My latest incarnation as teacher in general, and as kindergarten teacher in particular, is relatively recent. It arose from a desire to do something differ-ent (again) and to spend more time with the same group of children. It was also an attempt to answer questions generated during my previous two careers, as a worker with cognitively and physically challenged children and adults, and as a speech-language pathologist. Beyond this, however, it has been the latest step in an ongoing a quest to find out how best to foster such processes as imagining, organizing, understanding, and thinking. These processes are the core of what we so often say we want children to do, yet I frequently hear teachers complain that our children are lacking in these areas.

Certainly, this quest follows the work of Bloom (1956), who identified a whole series of processes he considered basic to the educational enter-prise. In a different way, Dewey (1966) and many who have followed him, such as Gardner (1983, 1991), Wells (1986), Costa (1991), and Sternberg (1985, 1988; Baron and Sternberg 1987) have concerned themselves with the issue of how to develop effective learners able to carry out their own inquiry. All these writers have been part of my own wondering as I have moved among different places and professional positions.

Over these two decades, I have encountered a range of learners besides Caroline whom I want to include as thinkers. My first experience was in a school for cognitively challenged learners in Winnipeg. The school was part of an institution for individuals with physical and cognitive disabilities and was entirely segregated. I worked first in the school and later in the occupational therapy department, and I was struck by the strengths and weaknesses of some of the individuals I met.

I can clearly remember an adolescent girl named Felicia, who moved her wheelchair with her one strong arm and hardly spoke. There was some question about whether she'd benefit from a current summer program. Yet she had a remarkable sense of order and organization. She quickly figured out when things were to be put away, and she knew where they went. How much she understood came home to me when one day she arrived early and began to set up the room and set out materials. She'd never done this before, nor had anyone ever shown her. As time went on, she actually put materials from her neighbor's area into that person's lap as a reminder to clean up. After a while, one could hardly remember how the program ran without her. She hardly spoke and appeared to have limited ability to process language yet she could do far more than anyone expected. How did she understand, and how did we so badly underestimate her? I also wonder from the distance of the years if there wasn't more to be made of her ability.

Around this same time I had one of my more adventurous teaching experiences. We were trying to teach Barry, a young lad, to cross the road, a sparsely traveled road leading into the institution. Certainly, he'd had limited exposure to roads in this institutional setting and needed to be better prepared for the larger community. Most of us have had the experience of patiently teaching someone a series of steps and seeing them acknowledged, repeated, and practiced—only to have our teaching fail utterly in a real test. Each time a car would come by, we'd ask Barry what he was going to do. He'd give the right answer, but then invariably, he would take a step into the road. An onlooker would have sworn we were teaching Barry how to get himself run over. My career had been quite short to that point, and so it took very little time for the whole of my career to flash before my eyes, a good thing, since Barry kept having to be stopped.

This would have been really frustrating except for the fact that Barry had immense personal charm. He was one those kids whom everyone knew and who knew everyone. He was skilled, even with limited language, in getting people to take him to lunch and buy him Cokes, and in general, provided enthusiastic company. Looking back, I wonder if he cared at all about crossing that road. After all, there was no one he knew on the other side, and on his side we were being quite animated. What if there had been someone on the other side he wanted to meet? Would he have solved the problem more quickly?

I have dozens of such stories from these years. They prompted my interest in two issues. First, I felt that language was critical to thinking. If only some of these learners could speak more and understand more, I truly believed that their learning would rise exponentially. Further, I was intrigued by the ways in which language serves to increase personal and social power. It was my perception that learners who were more linguistically able managed themselves better and received a more equitable response. Naturally, there were many exceptions (perhaps even in the very stories I have just told), but eventually I went back to school for a graduate degree in Human Communications Disorders. I then got a job in Edmonton that entailed consulting throughout northern Alberta. I was to provide advice and support for teachers who had learners ranging from preschool to adolescence with severe language and communication problems. The nature of this position put me into contact with fascinating children and wonderful teachers. It was certainly an opportunity to observe language and communication in all its forms. The work also demanded a certain level of practicality, because busy teachers would still have the child on Monday morning when I would be somewhere else. I was never the kind of speech-language pathologist who worked on articulation by withdrawing children from the class.

One of the children I remember best was a boy named Troy. I met him in a northern Alberta community as a preschooler. He had begun speaking very late (at the age of three) and was about to go to school having been talking for only a year and a half. I spent time with both Troy and his mother at their home. He was bright-eyed and very sociable, but it was clear that he hadn't been talking for long. In addition, he hadn't walked until he was past two years old and he was uncoordinated for his age. Toward the end of the exploratory interview, I casually asked his mother whether he had any interests or favorite playthings.

"Blocks," she said. "He loves his alphabet blocks." I asked to see these blocks and Troy got them. "What's he like to do with these blocks?", I asked, but I didn't need to. Before my eyes, he spelled "BLOCKS."

I asked for a warm-up of my coffee. (It is always prudent to have a little more coffee when you are calmly scrambling to think of what to say next.) Meanwhile, Troy was spelling "COFFEE" and was clearly distressed at only having one "F" to use. I wrote another "F" on my paper, gave it to him, and inquired further about how long this had been going on.

"He started doing this around the time he began to talk," she replied. It turned out that he could come close to spelling almost anything (although he needed more blocks). It also turned out that he could do hundred-piece jigsaw puzzles. Over the years, the challenge became how to teach him to *understand* what he was spelling and reading because of this tremendous ability. Even now, I wonder if we ever really thought of enough ways to use this strength. How could I suggest developing an ability I didn't possess to nearly the degree he did? It struck me then, and stays with me now, that he thought about the world in ways that were different from most of us around him.

At a later point in my life as a speech-language pathologist, I worked in a children's mental health treatment center. There I met Richard, a learner with what might be called "rigid tendencies." He loved to make up rules for everything. For example, he made a rule about speaking English on one floor of his house and another language on the next. Why did he make this rule?

"Because it was a different floor," he replied.

"What would happen if there was a third floor?" I asked.

"There is no third floor," he said with unerring logic.

However, one of the clever teachers I worked with had an idea: teach him rules for being flexible. He was taught to move his body flexibly, to spell inventively, to estimate profusely, and to think socially—all according to the rules. Naturally, there are limits to this type of approach, since some things are not so easily defined by rules, but we did use his understanding of the world to extend his thinking—and our own. I wondered if we could do this kind of teaching with all children and how far it would take us if we could.

Beyond this, however, it was clear that although I had become a speech-language pathologist to develop and extend the power of language, I kept running across children who seemed to think very well in ways that did not require language. This presented new puzzles.

I have described some of the more exotic variations on learning: learners who can read but have difficulty understanding, people who are rigidly logical, children who are so incredibly sociable you know they'll make it in life despite other weaknesses. Most educators have probably met them all as well as many others. One by one, they can be puzzling, but what if they are all in the same class together? This isn't a joke, since many different kinds of learners, with a range of needs and strengths, are usually in the same class together. How do we teach a basic curriculum let alone consider the deeper questions of thinking? Already we too often feel as if we're scrambling just to keep up.

I want to do more than just keep up in the classroom. I want to get ahead—or at least to stay focused while I'm falling behind. I use two basic strategies: asking questions and setting challenges. These are the same strategies I use to keep my students thinking. There is no point in seeing myself as all that different from those I teach. I wonder about their learning and they wonder about it, too. This perspective keeps me anchored in the reality of everyday teaching and learning and helps develop a common bond between us in the classroom.

Like any teacher, I ask myself questions all the time. Some days I just wonder where I put my attendance folder, or my pen, or that book I meant to read to the class. Other days, I wonder why a class is staring at me as if I've just spoken about an unfathomable mystery of the universe, when I was sure we were discussing the alphabet. In both situations, a good question may allow me to articulate what I'm feeling. It may also generate a plan of action. So I can ask which one of the giggling children took my attendance folder or I can decide it's a good time to inquire about the students' understanding of the lesson. At a deeper level, I can wonder about a better system for keeping track of the attendance folder or imagine better ways of teaching the alphabet.

For children, a well-timed question can provide focus to an activity. Asking John if it matters that the large blocks are at the top may give him a moment to reflect on previous constructions that have fallen down. A question can also be an invitation; sometimes I ask children what they were thinking about during a story. Beyond the questions themselves I want to provide challenges. A challenge is meant to take us on the next step of the journey. It can be wondering about improbable things. The other day, for example, I wondered if Caroline could draw a picture of her imagination. She couldn't, but she made up a song about it with another child. ("Purple rain, purple rain, from my brain, from my brain.") It can also be establishing criteria, such as making a bridge strong enough for the plastic animals to stand on or creating problems by changing the password on a computer and seeing what happens. But some challenges I return to over and over. These are the ones that keep me focused, and not surprisingly, they provide an underlying dynamic for many of the following chapters.

To create a classroom environment in which everyone *can improve in his or her thinking.*
I keep being puzzled by students who fit into one framework but not another: one who could apparently read but not speak, another who could create geometric designs but not (yet) name any letters of the alphabet, and still another who had a burning passion to find out what happened to the Titanic—all three were members of my kindergarten class one year. This is a common occurrence for many of us these days. The emotional, social, academic, and cognitive range of our students is complex, and we often have curricula that explicitly address only some of the needs of learners. To move ahead, we need frameworks that not only account for these children but give us some way of devising environments and teaching practices to accommodate them.

To create an environment in which all students want to think and see themselves as thinkers.
It's all very nice to postulate a framework for intelligence, but students need more than that to motivate them to think. Many teachers and students tell me how much students hate to take risks, ask questions, and challenge themselves. It's also true that we, as teachers, can fall into the same trap. Creating an inquiring classroom is not easy. A few years ago, for instance,

I had a very lively fifth/sixth-grade class full of larger-than-life students. One such student, Aisha, complained that I often returned student questions with "I don't know, that's a good question. I wonder how you could find out?"

"Man, you never answer questions. But you always wonder about this and wonder about that." She said the word *wonder* with a lot of "attitude."

"Well, that's how people learn," I replied. "Remember how I had you practice asking questions early in the year? You have to keep asking questions in order to learn."

She sat silent for a second and then her eyes widened. "You mean I gotta ask questions *every single day?!* Oh my God, I'm gonna *die!*"

If this realization seems a little slow in coming, consider that for many students it never happens at all. (If it also seems that this class should have had their own television series, I am inclined to think you may be right.) Sure, I had the class do independent projects based on their own questions, and we practiced asking different types of questions. Still, the value of asking questions might not have occurred to Aisha either if she had not finally noticed that I asked myself questions and talked about questions all of the time.

To create a classroom where the everyday acts of teaching and learning lead to thinking.
I don't have time to take on many new projects or integrate much new material into my teaching. I don't want strategies to be "added on" to my program even if I'm the one making the additions. It would feel forced and very quickly lead to the problem of setting aside a time during which we would "think." This would be false and artificial, and it would create more problems than it would resolve.

The challenge is to cover the curriculum in ways that raise the level of the students' thinking. To get more from my teaching, I keep looking at the basic, everyday stuff—asking questions, writing stories, organizing a notebook, painting a picture—and wonder if I have gotten the most from these routine acts of teaching.

To have a curriculum that seriously addresses children's need to think about electronic media and popular culture.
So often these days I hear teachers lament that children today don't have the attention span or the imagination they did ten, fifteen, or twenty years ago. Indeed, I also hear it from parents and read it in the popular press.

Blame for this is often laid on the media—video and computer games, toys, television, and so on. I come up against the powerful influence of the media in children's thinking all the time. Popular culture enters the classroom uninvited: a class frightened that a suspended classmate will come back and shoot them, students who make a television set and just pretend to "watch" it, and paintings of the logo of a popular series of books for older children. I don't think we should fight this influence so much as learn to use it to prompt critical and creative thinking in children.

In the next chapter I'll explore some the work of some of the theorists of thinking, particularly Howard Gardner. Over the course of the book I hope to illustrate some of the strategies and techniques that have worked for me in creating thinking classrooms. Although much of the text reflects my recent experiences in teaching kindergarten, the ideas and techniques are equally applicable to older students. Indeed, I first tried many of them with older students and then adapted them for younger children. Someday, after all, I hope to earn that penny.

2

Beginning Answers

It was the eyes that were memorable. They were dark, peering out from under thick eyebrows and, it seemed, never missing anything. They were expressive eyes, showing a whole range of emotions. As a learner, Sam had some difficulty with language and with "remembering things." I had traveled a long way to do an assessment in a remote part of the country, and the first thing that struck me was the intelligence of his eyes. He was open, even enthusiastic at times, and loved to move around. It also seemed clear that he couldn't remember the names of things. He referred to everything as a "something." "This something tastes good," he said about a bag of potato chips, or "This 'something' is a good 'something,' " about a megaphone. In some ways, the problem was obvious. What no one told me was that Sam had his own solution.

In those days, I was interested in collecting a sample of a child's spoken story by having the child go through a wordless picture book and then retell the story to me in some fashion or another.

Sam was having none of that.

He looked amiably enough through the book, which was, as I recall, one of the old Mercer Mayer's Boy, Dog, Frog series. However, when it came time to tell his story, he started by saying, "Me and my brother go fishing." Then he jumped up on the table and proceeded to mime himself and his brother fishing. It was no ordinary performance, but quite elaborate in its detail. I knew they were fishing, where the fishing can was, how big the worms were, and that they had traveled a long way to get the fish. Occasionally he spoke, to add something to the story. At one point, he broke into a song that (I think) he and his brother were singing on the boat. At another, while portraying the fish that got away, his movements came very close to dance. At the end of it all I clapped and he bowed, eyes ablaze with the joy of telling a story.

And then I wondered how I was supposed to rate this story in terms of other stories I had heard. Of course I couldn't. I needed a whole new framework.

Frameworks for explaining thinking are many and varied. Some take a very skill-oriented approach to thinking, while others view thinking as a collection of performances on specific tasks. We are often bombarded with new theories about what constitutes thinking and what schools and children have to do in order to think better. There are taxonomies, such as that of Bloom and Guilford, which analyze thinking as a complex collection of processes (Bloom 1956; Guilford 1967). Piaget, and many other researchers, have examined the developmental aspects of thinking. Still others, such as Flavell and his colleagues (1995), have examined the development of thinking from the perspective of meta-cognition—thinking about thinking. Many of these theorists have helped me to articulate some of what I see going on in children, and their influence will be evident in the following chapters.

MULTIPLE INTELLIGENCES

It is Howard Gardner's theory of multiple intelligences (1983) that I start from and return to in constructing my teaching practice. It accounts for the broadest range of learners and the most diverse ways of functioning. Briefly, Gardner suggests that there are eight distinct ways of knowing and representing the world, each an intelligence unto itself with its own unique rules, codes, and symbols. A learner who is proficient in a particular intelligence understands its *forms,* or symbols, and can apply them to make new *meanings.* These intelligences manifest themselves in different ways, however, depending on one's cultural background.

1. *Bodily-kinesthetic*

   An understanding of movement; creating and understanding meaning through movement.

Common domains/disciplines: sports, dance, intricate handwork.

Common skills: moving in a coordinated fashion and imitating a movement.

2. *Linguistic*

An understanding of language; creating and understanding meaning through language.

Common domains/disciplines: many forms of writing, poetry, speaking.

Common skills: understanding grammatical rules, speaking a different language, creating new stories.

3. *Logical-mathematical*

An understanding of highly organized, logical, and rule-based systems; applying these systems to create and understand meaning. This intelligence also includes creating and understanding number systems.

Common domains/disciplines: working with computers, mathematics.

Common skills: working with numbers, personal organization.

4. *Visual-spatial*

An understanding of visual and spatial symbols; creating and understanding meaning through visual and spatial symbols.

Common domains/disciplines: painting, sculpture, geometry.

Common skills: forming mental images, recognizing visual patterns.

5. *Musical*

An understanding of musical symbols; creating and understanding meaning through musical symbols.

Common domains/disciplines: composing, performing of all kinds, musical criticism.

Common skills: remembering songs, playing an instrument, reading musical notation.

6. *Interpersonal*

An understanding of the social world; creating and understanding meaning through the social world.

Common domains/disciplines: sociology, coaching or counseling, teaching.

Common skills: making a group work better, understanding society.

7. *Intrapersonal*

An understanding of intrapersonal symbols; creating and understanding meaning through intrapersonal symbols.

Common domains/disciplines: philosophy, psychology, religion.

Common skills: personal reflection, meditation.

8. *Naturalist*

An understanding of the natural world; creating and understanding meaning through the natural world.

Common domains/disciplines: botany, biology, zoology.

Common skills: identifying wildlife, growing plants, making fine distinctions between animals.

Gardner's methodology was to draw on data from a large range of sources, including "prodigies, gifted individuals, brain-damaged patients, *idiots savants,* normal children, normal adults, experts in different lines of work, and individuals from diverse cultures" (Gardner 1983, p. 9). Originally, he listed seven intelligences. Over the years, various arguments have been put forward in support of this or that new intelligence. Gardner has himself added the eighth, that of the naturalist, only recently.

The Appeal of This Approach

What I particularly appreciate about Gardner's work is that he has tried to go beyond this framework to discuss the creative and practical uses of his theory, and many of these practical applications inform this book. A number of other theories about thinking also have some appeal.

Edward de Bono (1973), one of the most prolific writers on thinking, merits a category unto himself. He has worked with everyone from school-children to business people and popularized such terms as "lateral thinking"—looking at an old problem in creative new ways. I enjoy his meditations on the nature of language and how to escape some of its limitations. For example, his ideas about brainstorming solutions to problems always incorporate what de Bono called "po": an invitation to think laterally and creatively.

Reuven Feuerstein (1979) devised a program to boost academic and intelligence test performance in learners with cognitive delays. It was his contention that such performance was based more on abstract contexts than on actual abilities. If learners had significant exposure to precise uses of language and reasoning, he believed they would demonstrate significant improvement in performance. His program, which he termed "instrumental enrichment," included strategies like stopping to talk through the problem—abstract, out-of-context geometric patterns—comparing it to other, similar problems, and using the processes of deduction and inference to achieve the best answers.

In the 1980s, Robert Sternberg (1985, 1988) launched his attack on I.Q. testing and generated his own model of intelligence, which he calls a *triarchic* model because it involves three components. His major criticism has always been that I.Q. measures only the analytical aspect of intelligence, which he refers to as the ability to compare and contrast, analyze, judge, and evaluate (Sternberg 1996, p. 149). However, he goes on to argue, this aspect of thinking is not the same as creativity, which is the ability to synthesize ideas, make connections, and look at old ideas with new ways and new ideas in old ways. This type of thinking is entirely different from analytical skills, and some people are better at thinking creatively. Sternberg also makes the argument for a "practical" intelligence, which is the ability to get things done in the real world, to size up new situations and adapt to them. These last two forms of thinking are not accounted for at all in traditional testing procedures, which penalize some and gives a false impression of the possible range of intelligence. This, in turn, leads to narrower teaching.

Daniel Goleman (1995) has recently published a successful book on what he calls "emotional intelligence." His argument is that we have gotten away from understanding the importance of managing and adapting one's feelings to the situation at hand, a skill that he considers critical to lifelong success. He marshals all kinds of data to support the idea that everything from delaying gratification to coping with stress is more critical than more traditional notions of intelligence. If one cannot manage emotions, how is one going to use any other intelligence in real-world situations? Like Sternberg, Goleman contends that traditional notions of assessment don't match up all that well with practical, real-world thinking.

Finally, there is L. S. Vygotsky, a major theorist of the social sciences, who worked in the Soviet Union in the late 1920s and early 1930s. Because he died young, at age 37, he did not have the chance to finish much of what he started. He, too, concerned himself with a wide range of subjects, from creativity to language learning in children with differing cognitive abilities. His work has influenced my thinking in subtler ways than has Gardner's. It is Vygotsky who contributed the notion that assessment is a dynamic dialogue, and in a broader sense, that the cultural context of an assessment matters. Probably his best known construct, however, is the "zone of proximal development." For Vygotsky, this "zone" represents not only what a child knows but also what a child is capable of understanding with the help of a more skilled peer or an adult. This is the critical question in any assessment: how much help did I give, how did I give that help, and what happened as a result of that help? This kind of help has been called scaffolding, which alludes to the temporary supports we give to assist the growth of a learner.

It is Gardner's theory that most appeals to me and, I think, to a lot of other teachers, for several reasons.

First, it is universal—it applies to adults as well as to children. Intelligences develop over the life span; indeed, they emerge more clearly as we get older. Being able to perceive similarities between our learners and ourselves helps to foster a sense of community and continuity in the classroom.

Gardner's theory of multiple intelligences is also universal in that it includes all learners. I have always found it possible to articulate the strengths of any learner within a multiple intelligences framework. It allows me to better—and more appropriately—value the very different learners I have met as a speech-language pathologist and teacher. Gardner's framework thus meets one of my main teaching criteria, which is that everyone is a thinker. It is also easy to remember because it has a certain kind of common-sense appeal. In a busy classroom the teacher can't see everything all the time, so a broad, easily applied framework is helpful in deciding where to focus.

In addition, it gives me new ways to explain thinking to students, so that even young children can understand the basic ideas and participate in the construction of their own knowledge of thinking. This fulfills one of my basic challenges: creating a classroom in which all children can see themselves as thinkers. I can then make credible claims about their abilities. Paulo can be seen as having great "smarts" when he makes patterns, Jonathon when he fixes the computer, and Blaine as a master builder. In this kind of environment, students with special needs can see themselves— and be seen by classmates—as having unique abilities. A student in a wheelchair, for example, can be admired for being able to drive the wheelchair (anyone who has ever tried to navigate any kind of wheelchair will know how difficult it is).

Finally, Gardner's theory allows me to make usable predictions in a classroom context. While not forcing children into a rigid framework, I can anticipate the kinds of performances and products that will engage them. Awareness of children's individual and collective strengths makes it is easier to individualize the program.

Cautions

As useful as Gardner's theory is, however, it does have its flaws. The most significant one is that it can be used to reduce the complexity of a learner's thinking to a single intelligence. Analyzing a learner in terms of one or two major intelligences is seductive, and to be sure, I have done it myself. Yet, in any learner, the intelligences weave together in a tapestry to link inner and outer worlds. The tapestries are alive and continually seeking ways to express and extend themselves. It is true that some intelligences may be stronger than others, but cognition tends to draw them together rather than apart.

Take the case of reading. On the one hand, it is a linguistic task, yet I have known many children who learned to read but still had significant difficulties with spoken language. At the same time, reading has a strong visual-spatial aspect. It can be very rhythmical, and some learners approach it from this perspective. It can also be approached in a very analytical, step-by-step way. Reading has strong qualities of interpersonal intelligence, and a consistent case has been made that very few children learn to read unless *someone* has repeatedly read to them. Without the self-confidence that results from perceiving oneself as a reader, children don't learn to read.

So which intelligence do learners demonstrate when they read successfully? In the end, all of them. Certainly a learner may have relied on some intelligences more than others to accomplish this task. The peril lies in making judgments too quickly and too simplistically. Thinking is a complex, endlessly changing set of processes. The larger difficulty is that so many individuals have jumped on the bare bones of Gardner's theory without taking the time to understand the larger scope of his work. It is important to see this work in the context of a set of broader interests.

THE BROADER PERSPECTIVE OF THE THEORY OF MULTIPLE INTELLIGENCES

Gardner's work consists of at least four interconnected strands. Each can be seen as separate, but inevitably, they intertwine to produce some of his most original and important ideas. First, Gardner has always had a strong interest in the development of artistic and creative talent. In this connection he was a founding member of Project Zero, a research program that attempts to document what creativity is. He was also a founding member

of Arts Propel, an organization advocating and documenting the best practices in arts education. It is within this framework that Gardner has ad-
dressed the role of the electronic media in creativity. As he outlined some
years ago in *Art, Mind, and Brain,* "the charge that television destroys or
reduces imaginative powers is largely unfounded" (1982, p. 262). Antici-
pating the kind of research more commonly done now, Gardner wondered
if exposure to the tools of television production would enhance children's
understanding of the medium. (I will look at examples of this kind of work
in later chapters.) More recently, he has compared the effects of video and
print on understanding (1997).

Second, Gardner has demonstrated a continuing interest in the neurosci-
ences and has carried out research on adults with neurological difficulties.
He has contributed to journals that report on aphasia.

Third, he has shown continuing interest in the cognitive sciences in general. Some of his earliest work attempted to place pioneers such as Piaget
in a historical context (1981). He has also written about children's use of
metaphor (1981), the relation of metaphor to thinking (Winner and Gardner 1993), the connections between the arts and cognition, and the impact
of electronic media on cognition (1982).

Finally, and most important, Gardner has taken an active role in arguing
about the need for extensive educational reform. Here, the various strands
of his work come together. In *The Unschooled Mind* (1991), Gardner outlines the serious shortcomings of the schooling process in creating true
thinkers. As one example of these shortcomings, he begins by citing fascinating research about the difficulty of university-educated adults in describing the scientific basis for the changing of the seasons. Many of
them reverted to explanations more typical of much younger learners, for
example, the earth moves farther away from the sun. He continues with
examples showing that "schooling" never quite resulted in "education," demonstrating the startling lack of critical thinking in political leaders, popular media figures, and among academics. He points out how often
we learn whole sets of facts we don't really understand and promptly forget. Gardner's question becomes why this is so and what to do about it.

Most learners, he argues, have simple, basic notions of how the world
operates that are formed by about the age of five. He marshals evidence
from a range of sources to document young children's view of how learning occurs and their concepts of math and language. When these "intuitive" learners (pp. 85–86) come to school, however, these notions
are not extended, challenged, or examined. Instead, we lay on what
we, as adults, consider it important for children to know. In this way, we

try to fit a body of knowledge on a base prepared for something entirely different.

Museums and Portfolios

Gardner understands the difficulty of educational change and acknowledges the challenges of trying to run a school based on the multiple intelligences perspective, especially given the demands this approach makes on teachers (1991, pp. 137–142). To this end, he has been involved in attempting to formulate an idea of how schools that actually educate the intelligences might look and has worked with teachers in different settings to create practical material applications of the theory. The work of Project Spectrum (of which he is founder) is one source for ideas that are actually used with young children. There is also the Key School in Indiana, an elementary school that began when a group of teachers actually wanted to apply his theory.

Drawing on the work of such centers, Gardner has begun to articulate his vision of what constitutes excellent practice. Some of his conclusions will not surprise progressive educators. He advocates classrooms well equipped with a wide range of materials, where assessment is holistic in nature and approaches like whole language and whole math are endorsed. One of his most striking ideas is that schools should resemble interactive museums, where children and mentors can meet. As he points out, such places have always been sites where creative, risk-taking inquiry occurs naturally. He quotes Lawrence Oppenheimer, the founder of The Exploratium, an interactive museum in San Francisco: "No one flunks museum" (1991, p. 201). He has also outlined proposals for a fairer system of ongoing assessment of a learner's potential, and it is here that his background in the arts shows through. He believes that we need to take into account learners' products, ranging from stories to sculpture, and their performances in everything from dance to debate. All this, he argues, needs to become part of a portfolio of work that an individual carries along over the course of his or her career as a learner. This process permits learners to review and reflect on their work.

Entry Points

At the same time, Gardner doesn't advocate teaching to the intelligences directly. Rather, he describes what he calls "entry points" that "map onto" and incorporate all the intelligences. Gardner (1991, 1993b) likens them to different doors to a room that represents the idea, concept, or subject being taught. Showing learners where the doors are and offering them ready access increases opportunities for using all the intelligences. The entry points he outlines include:

Stories are the narrative framework for any subject. History can be approached through story, as can art, music, or sports. In fact, I have yet to come up with a topic that can't be approached through story. Stories relate most obviously to language and linguistic intelligence, but they can also be told through music, movement, and the visual arts. For many teachers stories are a powerful and familiar entry point but so common that we often forget their tremendous power for many learners to integrate and create personal meaning. One of the challenges I have encountered in my teaching has been to create a program on thinking from daily classroom work. Stories obviously fit that description.

Experiential learning obviously encompasses a broad range of learning opportunities: science experiment, building a model of a castle door, or creating a game in response to a book are all examples. The idea of an authentic project through which participants construct knowledge in some fashion has been around for some time. Again, this sort of teaching occurs in so many classrooms, its impact on generating and expressing thinking may be underestimated.

A common synonym for experiential learning is "hands-on" learning, which suggests the core symbol system involved here. But experiential learning can also take place through musical (constructing an instrument), logical-mathematical (a trip to a science museum), or visual-spatial (building a bridge) symbol systems.

Logical-quantitative is a numerical, quantitative, and procedural approach to a subject that should be familiar from doing inventories, taking surveys, breaking events down into logical steps, and measuring and comparing sizes. It is an entry point to virtually any subject, and like stories and hands-on work, it is so common in schools and in the culture as a whole that it is worth going back over again. Still, it is possible to so trivialize a subject with data that thinking becomes impossible. The challenge is to have children use this entry point to gain insight into the topic and into the nature of logic and mathematics.

Aesthetics involves looking at the sensory and surface features of a subject. Color, shape, and dimension all come into play, as do ideas of balance, tone, and harmony. This entry point can range from the music of a particular culture to the morphology of animals to aspects of balance (an aesthetic concept) in a political system. It is probably used less often in all its possibilities but still arises naturally in many themes and studies. This entry point may be most successful among those with more "artistic" inclinations, although the arts cover all the intelligences.

Foundational (philosophical) is an entry point that explores the basic premises of a topic, including the fundamental questions of how and why. Wondering how people think and computers "think," speculating about God, arguing about right and wrong or fair and unfair are issues that come up in every school at every grade level and may involve creating formal philosophical arguments. It is particularly important because it is probably the least used entry point, yet the one most driven by the personal concerns of young children. While inherently intrapersonal, it touches on other symbol systems, such as language, and on interpersonal concerns, such as fairness.

Rigid, intelligence-by-intelligence, thinking-skill-by-thinking-skill teaching makes me uncomfortable, and the entry points have presented me with many new possibilities. Gardner envisioned these entry points as most useful to older students approaching more serious, discipline-specific subject matter. This is an appealing idea, but I think Gardner may have underestimated their power and their usefulness for young children. From an early age, young children use these entry points to explain their world. They tell stories to remember experiences and convey meaning. They count anything and everything as a way of analyzing the world and searching for order and pattern. They ask profound questions about the nature of reality. They are aware of the sensory and the aesthetic from the day they are born and spend much of their early lives trying to grasp ways to make the symbols meaningful. Finally, children are nothing if not practical, and they build, explore, and move in order to understand how the world works.

Furthermore, the skills and the learning required by these entry points constitute formidable thinking in their own right. Philosophy is based on questioning and inquiry; stories on knowledge of action, character, and time; aesthetics on experience with the sensory world, personal responsiveness, awareness of feelings, and familiarity with symbols of all kinds; the logical-quantitative on a range of sequential, numerical, and analytical skills. And working hands-on lets children truly figure out the inner workings of people, places, and things. A set of practices linking younger and older learners is common sense. If Gardner hasn't explicitly recognized this notion, it is at least implicit in his writing. He speaks, for example, of the power of inquiry from the earliest age and mentions the storytelling area in a Project Spectrum classroom as well as the naturalist corner. In these ways the foundations for the entry points are present early on.

The range of Gardner's ideas suggests many approaches to the challenges I outlined in the previous chapter. First, his work includes all learners so that learners with diverse abilities and skills can be perceived as having intelligence worth teaching in school. Teachers can respond by creating an environment that offers learning materials of all kinds, in recognition of different abilities.

The second challenge, getting all children to think and to see themselves as thinkers, encourages learners to feel that they are being taken seriously. Moreover, when children can demonstrate an insight others do not have, motivation increases. Thinking grounded in everyday teaching practice—whole language, whole math, and hands-on science—exists in many classrooms already as students ask questions, paint, tell stories, count, and explore.

The questions have been asked, and the directions given. Now it's time to consider practice.

RECOMMENDED READING

Gardner, Howard. *Art, Mind, and Brain: A Cognitive Approach to Creativity.* New York: Basic Books, 1982.

A pre-multiple intelligences book, this remains a very readable account of creativity. When I went back to it a few years ago, I found some excellent early research on the influence of television and electronic media on creativity.

———. *Frames of Mind: The Theory of Multiple Intelligences.* New York: Basic Books, 1983.

The classic work, easy to read and generally nontechnical. It is the original work that outlines the rationale and evidence for the intelligences. If you haven't read it, by all means do so. I have read the book a couple of times and certain sections many times. The book covers an enormous amount of material.

———. *The Unschooled Mind: How Children Think and How Schools Should Teach.* New York: Basic Books, 1991.

This is my favorite Gardner book. It offers a compelling critique of education, outlining the flawed thinking of adults in order to illustrate the failure of many of our present educational practices to encourage deep understanding. It also articulates a vision of what education might look like.

————. *Multiple Intelligences: The Theory in Practice—A Reader.* New York: Basic Books, 1993.

A collection of articles about approaches to multiple intelligences and the kinds of teaching practices that support these approaches. I found the material related to initiatives in arts education especially compelling.

3

Building Bridges:
The Role of Teachers

Sometimes you hear about what people you know are doing but it doesn't sink in. You know how it is. You're talking to someone and you ask how so-and-so is, and how their year is going. You mean to call but you just don't get around to it. Such was the case for me a few years ago. I had made the jump from speech-language pathologist to teacher, and I was very busy. Still, I remember asking someone how Anne Pietropaolo, a kindergarten teacher, and Bev O'Brien, a grade six teacher, were doing. "Oh," came the reply, "they're working together this year. They're into bridges—seriously into bridges." Now that comment should have been enough to inspire further inquiry, but the conversation moved on and I forgot about it.

In early July I happened to drive by the school where Anne and Bev work. In front of the building a large bridge had been constructed, very professional looking and solid, but I didn't make an immediate connection. I drove away thinking about something else, when suddenly it came back to me: "They're into bridges—seriously into bridges."

I didn't hear the whole story until much later, at a workshop they gave on how they built the bridge. They did so much, that the following synopsis is only a bare outline. Anne and Bev had worked together as grade one teachers and were looking for some way to reconnect so that their classes could interact. They wanted something more than the simple "reading buddies'' formula, and they also wanted to take into account the diverse needs of their students, including some who were new to Canada and spoke little English.

They tossed different ideas back and forth and eventually came up with the notion of *bridges*. They liked the idea because they could imagine a million possibilities for working together and enough content for both kindergarten and grade six. They envisioned making an actual bridge of some kind, although neither of them had ever done such a thing before, attracted by the range of metaphors it would encompass—a bridge between the grades, a bridge to learning, a bridge to community involvement.

They began the project by introducing their students to the idea of bridges. As they planned, Anne and Bev considered the different intelligences of the students. For example, they told the story of ''The Three Billy Goats Gruff,'' in which a bridge is a critical feature. In the gym the sixth graders made arches with their bodies and the smaller children went under them. They also looked at many pictures of bridges. In a particular stroke of genius, the two teachers hired a bus to drive around Toronto so the children could see many different kinds of bridges.

Bit by bit, a kind of magical synergy took over. It became one of those projects where almost everything goes right. An architect and then an engineer visited the school to discuss bridges with the children. A hardware company got involved, donating materials and expertise to the project, and employees also participated, even showing children how to swing a hammer. The children took a field trip to a design and technology center where teachers and students in our school board learn about constructing hands-on projects. Students met with school board and municipal officials to submit plans and receive approval, and a design by one of the students was eventually chosen for the actual bridge. A genuine sense of inquiry and collaboration developed between teachers and students and spilled over into the community. As the bridge was actually under construction on a couple of Saturdays, people stopped to watch, wield a hammer, and contribute food.

The bridge project is the single best application of Gardner's work I know of in a school setting. Authentic inquiry shaped the entire process. Anne and Bev used as entry points story, aesthetics, logical-quantitative thinking, and hands-on work. They taught students to value different ways of representing information. They involved genuine mentors from the local community. They built bridges in every sense.

BEGINNING WITH OURSELVES: THE INTELLIGENCE OF TEACHERS

All learners come to school seeking outlets for their intelligence. One of the teacher's major jobs is to ensure that children enjoy a wide variety of opportunities within the classroom to grow and develop. However, teachers themselves are also learners. We have our own need for success and our own varieties of intelligence that seek expression. Classroom environment, curriculum, and instructional strategies begin with us. We bring our own talents and passions to the classroom, and while these can be useful in mentoring children, they can also drive the way we set up the environment. We must be careful to acknowledge what we are good at—and what we are not.

Personal reflection is one of the cornerstones of any program concerned with thinking, and it has to start with us. If we do not wonder aloud in front of children and ask ourselves questions, how will they learn? It is worth remembering that asking questions is not as easy as we might think. One of my earliest experiences with reflective practice occurred in a university course where the weekly assignment was to ask a single question in response to a reading assignment. This was immensely challenging.

The work of theorists such as Hunt (1987) and Schön (1987) has convinced me that we need to articulate our own thinking and beliefs. This isn't easy, since our own thinking can be invisible to us and there are so many other ways to formulate our thoughts besides words. Yet understanding how we think is helpful for several reasons: we gain a better understanding of thinking in general—there is nothing like a real-world experience to make material come to life; we become more sensitive to the range of ways in which we think; and by knowing ourselves as learners and thinkers, we better understand what our students need.

Although I am not a poet or a fiction writer, I do like to tell stories. Storytelling is a key part of my repertoire, and I also love to hear stories of all kinds. I am good at remembering things visually and use a lot of visual imagery when I speak, but I'm not much for drawing or painting. I appreciate ideas that are logically laid out, but I'm not as strong at working with numbers and computation. I enjoy listening to many kinds of music, but I don't play an instrument, read music, or sing particularly well. I have excellent interpersonal skills, especially in small groups, but I often like to be alone. I love nature, but I live in the middle of a large city. I can be quite reflective, but there are also times when I'd rather go jogging than consider the day.

It is important for us to consider who we are when we enter the classroom. Part of the value of such an exercise is that it imparts a sense of the complexity of symbol systems within a single individual. More important, this range of intelligences can be a great help in developing these intelligences in children I teach. I have given time to language and storytelling for so long, it is hardly surprising that so many of the children I teach tell wonderful stories. My students also tend to have a sense of humor and a high regard for books. These are examples of where one teacher's natural passions can lead a class. But in setting up—and being part of—a classroom, I must also be aware that if making music is not a particularly strong aspect of my own musical intelligence, I need to ensure that a variety of musical materials are available and schedule time for music during the day. I need to invite others with more expertise into my classroom. I also have to let children with musical abilities lead the way: as is often the case, they know more songs—and sing them better—than I do.

THE TEACHER SETS THE ENVIRONMENT

Of all the things involved in organizing a thinking program, setting up the environment is probably the most important, because it is one of the primary bridges between teachers and learners and the curriculum. Is it any wonder, then, that in my own case, I have to be vigilant, and remind myself not to overlook the musical instruments in the corner? Our own intelligences as teachers may be invisible to us, but reveal themselves in how we set up a classroom and schedule our time. Take stock of your own environment. Are there materials and enough space to accommodate all the intelligences? Are they accessible all day or just some of the day? Are some materials, like those having to do with language and mathematics, more freely available? How well do students know how to use these materials? Does the program include structured time as well as opportunities for individual discovery?

Every classroom presents different possibilities and imposes different restrictions on how space is used. Every school and grade level likewise has its own requirements for scheduling and program organization. To be fair to all my students and their various languages of thinking, I attempt to integrate Gardner's (1991) idea of an "interactive museum," which he considers so critical to authentic teaching of different symbol systems. The image brings to mind a place of inquiry and exploration that challenges our learners and helps us as teachers to understand their conceptual processes.

So, at any point in the year, there are magnifying glasses and telescopes, frozen fish and lichens, computers and rocks in this or that corner of the classroom. There is always an array of materials and all kinds of paper for children to use as they wish. Occasionally, there are buckets of fresh snow, which we bring to a large water table. Children sculpt, construct, and color the snow and of course, watch it melt.

Beyond all this however, the environment is also affected by the kinds of learners and what is going on in the class. I try to keep things flexible—we rearrange desks and furniture seeking a balance between movement, social harmony, and good work space. A group of children interested in music and dance, for example, needs space for movement and improvisation. A group of reluctant readers, in contrast, needs an inviting, comfortable place for reading with lots of cushions, books, and magazines.

Figure 3 shows how my kindergarten class is presently set up. Balancing materials is a consideration, but it doesn't mean limiting certain areas to certain types of thinking. A program based on multiple intelligences does not require that a "center" or a particular section of the day or week be set aside for each intelligence. It would probably be difficult to sustain, but it would also falsely imply that the intelligences are somehow separate in the world.

Teacher as Information Broker

A reasonably well-equipped school offers materials to support most intelligences: gyms, musical instruments, books of all kinds, and so on. One of Gardner's (1993b) critical concepts is that of the teacher as a "broker of information." Basically, he suggests that learners need someone to nurture their intelligence and a "teacher" can direct the learner to resources, techniques, and people who can help develop that intelligence. Many teachers already do this, but Gardner's point is that we can and should do more of this kind of "brokering." A "teacher" can also be another student or an adult as well as the actual teacher. He also strongly advocates the use of mentors to support and extend learners' intelligence. It is a logical conclusion, since no one can know everything. There are limits to my ability to foster musical intelligence, for example, though I consciously attempt to get better every year by practicing and inviting others to demonstrate to the class.

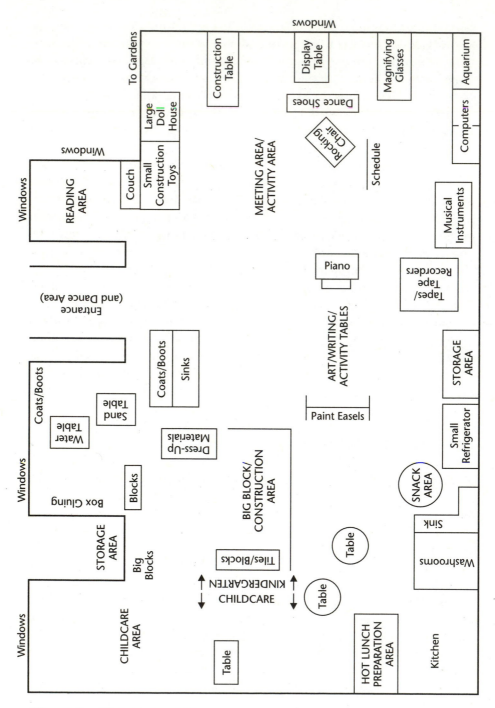

Figure 3   Classroom map

When Anne Pietropaolo and Bev O'Brien were planning their bridge project, they did exactly this kind of information brokering. They brought in mentors like the architect who showed slides of different kinds of bridges and provided feedback on some of the drawings children had done at different points in the process; and the engineer who demonstrated ways to make bridges stable. Even their trip to a large hardware building company provided opportunities—teachers and students learned to use the tools needed to build the bridge.

Similarly, when university students do practicum placements in my class, I make a point of asking them about any special abilities they might have that would enrich the classroom. Over the last couple of years, we've been fortunate in having people who speak different languages, people with a love of science, and, as I'll relate in Chapter 5, a dancer.

Teacher as Helper

In teaching—and assessing the results of our teaching—it is important that we stop to reflect on what we are doing. We need to ask ourselves how much help we have given to a learner, how we provided that help, and what happened as a result. It is also worthwhile to analyze whether our help was direct or indirect, since this indicates which approach is most effective with a particular child.

From a multiple intelligences perspective, it is also worth considering *how* we do the helping. Every domain and discipline requires its own kind of teaching. It may include giving a child specific directions, but can also include the direct contact of a mentor. A dancer, for example, might move one child's hand and reposition another child for optimal movement. When children in my class were learning to play the guitar, and struggled to master the fingering, the music teacher would actually stand behind them and finger the guitar with them. I have also watched physiotherapists working with learners who had significant motor impairments; as the therapist handled the child, the child became more competent at moving in different ways.

If you were to ask the dancer, the music teacher, or the physiotherapist about it, they might struggle for words. Prompted by their own (nonlinguistic) bodily-kinesthetic intelligence, they just knew what to do and "felt" the difference in the learner's response. This is one of the most powerful ways to teach and learn the "codes" of an intelligence: the child begins to learn the specific gestures required by the activity and receives the instruction through the "code" of movement. In this way children learn not only what it is to acquire a skill but also how to learn through the medium of the body.

Helping is not always this "hands-on," however, although I will return to physical contact later. More often, it involves some specific demonstration in the language of that discipline: a piece played on the guitar allows a learner to hear its "sound"; reading aloud from a pattern book demonstrates how language constructs a story; using a hammer models how to nail boards together to make a bridge.

Helping can also be less direct. New kinds of paper, new kinds of markers, a different set of art prints on the walls might be of far greater help to someone with visual-spatial intelligence than all the talking in the world. A dance video can present a whole new set of ideas about movement. Photographs of previous big block constructions can challenge children to try to make the exact same structure. A trip in a bus to look at different kinds of bridges raises children's awareness of all the possibilities.

It is worth reminding ourselves that multiple intelligences are not simple or straightforward, and different students move us to draw on different intelligences. Putting musical instruments in a less trafficked corner of the room can help a quieter child approach music, while another needs to be part of a group to become actively involved. Some children respond well to a verbal description of how to do something, while others do best when you move their hands through the appropriate motion. In a way, it's a bit like a dance, with one person leading and the other trying to match rhythms.

Teacher as Audience

I think back to a boy named Joseph, a quiet learner who had spent as much of the first three months of school at the computer as he could. One day, however, he slid over to the piano and sat quietly experimenting on the keys. I told him I liked what he was playing and asked if he was thinking about anything in particular. He shrugged. The next day he returned for a longer time. I remarked that he was playing longer today, or something like that. I was an audience for him and, in simple ways, encouraged him to develop what was an intelligence. Another child might have enjoyed the attention but been indifferent to the medium, but Joseph returned to the piano again and again. In time—and even with *my* feedback—he started to develop some elegant little experiments.

Sometimes we are not so much a dance partner as an audience. Serving as an audience for a child is another powerful teaching technique. It takes time, careful attention, and the occasional kind word, but such teaching is critical in a hurried world. The simple act of giving a child undivided attention can encourage an emerging passion and provide a catalyst for more independent steps. In this regard, I take a page from David Elkind's book, *The Hurried Child* (1981). It is aimed at parents but its message is one we need to keep in mind. We push children to "hurry up and develop"; we have little patience for those who develop more slowly. We do not sit back and let our teaching work. We do not wait for children to make discoveries on their own so that we may applaud them.

Now, it is true that teachers are hurried, too. We are under pressure to cover the curriculum in certain ways as never before. Yet despite this pressure—and maybe *because* of it—we try to make time for ourselves and our students to immerse ourselves in the subjects at hand. At Lambton Park, it is practically a maxim that even young children need an hour of uninterrupted time for their own self-directed activities. If we want children to have longer attention spans, then we must first be the ones to pay attention.

RECOMMENDED READING

Bodrova, Elena, and Deborah Leong. *Tools of the Mind: The Vygotskian Approach to Early Childhood Education.* Toronto: Prentice Hall, 1996.

This is the best book I know of on Vygotsky in the classroom. It is elegant and simple, and provides numerous classroom examples that demonstrate teaching and learning in a Vygotskian framework.

Ostrow, Jill. *A Room with a Different View: First Through Third Graders Build Community and Create Curriculum.* York, ME: Stenhouse Publishers, 1995; Markham, ON: Pembroke Publishers, 1995.

This book reminded me in many ways of the bridge-building project: the author, a teacher, created a year-long project that transformed her classroom into a tropical island and provided a framework for the year's learning. I especially recommend it to teachers who are tired of a "theme of the month" approach. It is also an impressive piece of work in that it outlines plausible ways of accommodating a multi-age group spanning four years.

Whitmore, Kathryn, and Caryl Crowell. *Inventing a Classroom: Life in a Bilingual, Whole Language Learning Community.* York, ME: Stenhouse Publishers, 1994.

This book is about the role of teachers in creating a classroom. I especially enjoyed the fact that the authors expand their teaching practice to include children who do not speak English as their first language. They emphasize the many ways in which language, literacy, and culture are invented and reinvented by teachers and learners.

4

From Structure to Construction

In my career I have known many cute and appealing children, but Jonathon probably tops them all. He is so engaging, he probably should come with a diabetic warning label. He demonstrates many kinds of intelligence but struggles to understand and use spoken language. When he entered kindergarten his difficulty had already been identified as well as the associated problems with changes of activity or routine and not being much of a risk taker.

I was using a system of taking attendance whereby a learner entering the classroom took a name card from the table and placed it in a board before sitting down. We then counted how many were and were not present. It is a very visual and concrete routine. With Jonathon in the class, however, I decided to take this visual organization a step further. I created a visual schedule with cards for each section of the day. Every day we reviewed the schedule for the day because it wasn't always the same. Our gym and library times varied, and they could change depending on whether or not we could go outside or a trip or special event had been planned. When an activity was over, we would turn over the card indicating that section of the day. We also looked at the date on the calendar, although calendars are only important when children have a reason to know the date. When ''needle day'' (measles immunization) was on the horizon, we began to cross out the days and count ahead. When it was over, we counted the days that had passed until it was a dim memory.

To say that Jonathon loved this schedule doesn't begin to capture how important it was to him. He would run into the room, muddy boots dripping, to check the schedule before he even took off his coat (not every routine was firmly established). He'd race to turn over the appropriate cards and became keenly aware if the schedule was wrong, for example, if cards that should have been turned over hadn't been.

As the year progressed, an interesting thing started to happen. A few children began to "play" with the schedule. One day the order of events was reversed to start with "going home." Eventually, the whole class, including Jonathon, started to play with the schedule. Cards were rearranged to make a whole day of activity time or a whole day of gym or to omit going home. The play spread to other routines, including the attendance board that kept track of who was present. Stuffed animals got name cards, as did adults. Other children's names appeared—"invisible children," they told me. The kindergarten class found all this hilarious. Better still, Jonathon knew it was funny, although he'd leap up to "fix" it as soon as he could.

Finally, on a Friday afternoon at the end of the year, Jonathon raced back to the schedule. I pointed that out that all the cards had been turned over, but he simply said, "Next week," as he turned them back for the week to come. It was the kind of thinking that, once achieved, can never go backward. In a very real sense, Jonathon had discovered the future.

THE NEED FOR STRUCTURE

All teachers establish some kind of structure in their program, and for good reason—it is inherent to teaching. Vygotsky makes the point that, by providing structure, a mediator enables another to achieve a level of performance he or she wouldn't achieve at that time alone. In doing so, the mediator shows the road ahead. In the case of learning to read and use the schedule in my kindergarten classroom, this was literally true. As children got comfortable with it, they began to anticipate what was to come. Mediators also provide the structure necessary to turn an interest into something more enduring. The point of checking our daily schedule was not to have

Figure 4   The schedule inspires a lot of writing. Here is Amy's version of what the schedule should be.

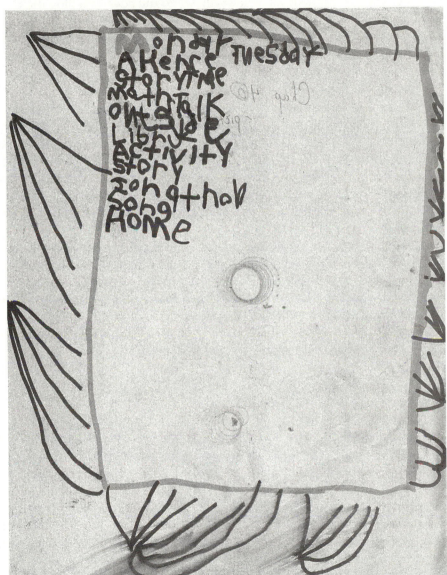

children follow it so that my day went better. It was one way of responding to their endless questions: What will happen today? What will happen first? When can we go to the gym? When will we go outside? Teaching the children about schedules channeled some of this interest into a deeper understanding of personal organization and time. Children began to make their own schedules for home. Faiza, for example, made a list of what foods should be eaten on what days (notably omitting her least favorite foods).

Structure obviously matters. The problem is *how much* direction to give. I sometimes worried that I would overdo the scheduling and discourage spontaneity. Knowing how direct or indirect to be is the decision teachers face every day. When we are very specific, children may know exactly what to do—but it takes away from their ability to make their own decision, to think for themselves, and, in the final result, to perceive themselves as "thinkers." Yet to be indirect is to leave to chance some of the knowledge that would enable learners to move forward quickly and exercise individual expression.

Howard Gardner has dealt explicitly with the issue of structure in relation to artistic development in *To Open Minds* (1989). When he went to China to study the educational system, particularly the arts curriculum, he found a system of highly structured, uniform instruction that could produce startling and dramatic results in even young children's art. The experience challenged his notions about creativity, which he had thought was better developed in open, more learner-directed settings.

Multiple Intelligences, Multiple Structures

I often struggle in trying to decide how much structure to provide children and when. Perhaps a multiple intelligences framework could help with this problem. The thrust of this theory is that all symbol systems merit direction in their own right. Moreover, these symbol systems weave together in different ways in any number of disciplines. Each discipline comes with its own structures, and these can take many forms. They can be physical routines to be mastered, like hanging up a coat in the same place or using the same brush stroke to paint; they can be patterns to be learned, understood, and mastered, like shapes seen again and again or sequences of notes heard over and over; and there are also "scripts," or sequences of words to be used in repeated and predictable ways: saying "good morning" to people is following a script and so is the superhero playing children love to replicate.

However, while there are many forms of structure, not all structure is equally valuable. Much of the structure in our schools goes hand in hand with teaching "measurable" skills. We love to quantify skills because we believe they allow us to detect improvement. What can be counted seems to make people feel better. Scores on standardized tests, achievement tests, and I.Q. tests can all be reduced to a number. Inevitably, once a numerical evaluation is established, any teacher, myself included, feels the pressure to teach in ways that will improve that number. By focusing too narrowly on disciplines that can be measured numerically, we overlook those areas that cannot. In turn, by focusing only on quantitative structure, we stop laying foundations for qualitative thinking. Thus, for example, the arts, social skills, emotional wellness, creativity, and personal reflection get second billing. Undervaluing these forms of structure is part of our overall cultural pattern of undervaluing some kinds of symbol systems.

Unfortunately, the results can be very personal. Without access to a range of structures, children may be left to figure out how to manage their emotions, express ideas artistically, or convey feelings through movement by themselves. In a world that complains about the lack of discipline in children, taking away the structures that might guide learners in organizing and focusing seems very odd indeed. In a special class I once taught for learners with behavioral and academic exceptionalities, for example, we began the day with basic seat work (just to get everyone sitting down), but we also had breakfast. Clearly, not everyone had eaten, but in addition, the smell and presence of food, the certainty of routine, was calming. There was no reason to be afraid—who can bomb out on eating breakfast?

More important, however, is that these children began to learn the step-by-step skills of cooking. Cooking is a structured way of nurturing oneself. It gave them a glimmer of the possibility that they were capable of managing themselves.

A learner in my kindergarten class had been described to me as a very quiet child who showed no particular interest in anything. This appeared to be true for the first two months of school. But one day, after many discussions and demonstrations of visual patterns on chart paper, she marched up to the chart and painted an elaborate design consisting of a crescent with the open side facing right, followed by two triangles and then a mirror image of the first crescent facing the other way. She understood not only pattern but symmetry as well! From that point on, she produced painting after painting at the paint center. When I asked her why she hadn't done so earlier, she said, "I never knew what to paint before."

Teachers and Structure

Restricting structure to what is measurable also has an impact on teachers. All teachers use some form of structure, in their daily routines if nowhere else. However, by rewarding and acknowledging only those structures that produce measurable results, we give the impression that some of our other daily activities are merely the stuff we do before we teach. This is cause for concern, because this is one area where teachers do very well. What is predictable is safe and secure. Our ordinary daily routines can encourage calm, even temperaments. Furthermore, by making these routines visible in the form of schedules, we let children see what is coming and when, which can calm an individual learner like Jonathon as well as a whole class.

At the same time, undervaluing our daily routines leads teachers to complain about the unexpected interruptions that can throw the day's plan into chaos so that we don't get to "the curriculum." This, too, is a disservice, because such interruptions are often the most "teachable" moments. Such moments range from learning how to cope with an emotional upset to how to deal with life's little emergencies. Here we can introduce children to different kinds of routines for self-management: When you are hungry, this is a safe way to get some food for yourself. If you are upset, find a way to calm down. If you are cut, get a Band-Aid. If it is a serious emergency, call 911.

Teachable moments can also be instances when teachers deliberately create a problem. I have induced mass panic in my students by insisting that they look for patterns within the multiplication tables. I then compounded their panic by refusing to tell them how to solve the problem and by insisting that they brainstorm possible solutions before they actually attempted to solve it. Some suggestions were creative—call in the child welfare authorities—but others were more reasonable, like talking with a friend or making the chart bigger so patterns would be easier to spot.

It is often more productive simply to create problems and then teach children how to cope with the unexpected. This forces them to apply old ideas and actions in new contexts. It also keeps teachers in charge of some of the teachable moments and lets us anticipate the problem-solving strategies children might use. Creation, invention, and discovery follow from such problem-solving environments.

The daily discussions in my classroom about the schedule were really problem-solving opportunities of one kind or another. On occasion, I would put a new card, such as "performance," into the schedule. As soon as the children entered the room, we would discuss what the new card could be. They would exchange ideas based on the shape of the word, the initial letters, and anything I might have recently said. Once they had figured out what the actual word was, they would try to figure out what it meant. If they noticed that there were few items on the schedule that day, it was a clue that something "big" was going to happen. I would help by acknowledging answers that were more on target, giving hints, and eventually answering questions about what a performance was, where it would take place, and how long it was.

NEGOTIATING STRUCTURE: A GRASSROOTS CURRICULUM

Structure shouldn't be a "we lead them" or "they lead us" kind of paradigm. Learners need to have enough *shared* control of a pattern, script, or routine so that they feel a sense of partnership with both the teacher and the tool. For example, reading was on the schedule every day, yet there were many occasions when the class would vote on whether to extend indoor activity time or go outside. The schedule was a living document, not a set of rules. This, in the end, is one of the key differences between structure that reduces creativity and structure that enhances it. Structure has an even greater impact when children are a part of the process. Having the class participate in the schedule making extended some control to them. More important, however, it was a forum for negotiation. The schedule provided a common language with which we could discuss the day.

In their wonderful book *Constructing Knowledge Together: Classrooms as Centers of Inquiry and Literacy,* Wells and Chang-Wells (1992) make the case that "education is dialogue" (p. 32). In one sense, this means a dialogue about problems in these teachable moments, and their book is full of examples about such moments in science. At a deeper level, they point out that through these dialogues the teacher can discover what interests and motivates students and discern the "current state of understanding of individual students." This information, in turn, lets teachers know what structure, skill, or attitude may be needed to take student's thinking to the next level.

Negotiation is more than a daily practice, it is a whole way of teaching. Demonstrating scripts, patterns, and routines occurs in a kind of turn-taking exchange. Sometimes it is my turn to make a move, either by teaching a new structure or by letting children take over an existing one. This happened when I taught children how to use the daily schedule and then let them take control over it. At other times it is the children's turn to make a move when they need a new structure they haven't had before. For instance, teaching the children about calendars became a priority when "needle day" loomed ahead.

I would not pretend that I am perfect at recognizing the need for a new structure. But trying to live in tune with the natural rhythms of a classroom is in the end a more realistic way of covering any curriculum through different symbol systems. I did not, for example, wake up one morning and decide that children should have an interest in the deeper implications of media and technology. It's just that the subject kept coming up in the classroom. It informed storytelling, drawing, play, toys, homework, deep-seated fears, and feelings of self-worth. How could I not try to put some structure in place that would lead to greater comprehension?

A *grassroots curriculum* is an image I take from Cassidy and Lancaster (1993). They outline a system for charting and keeping track of the children's interests. I haven't mastered this kind of charting, but I do use my anecdotal notes to keep track of individual and class trends in play, book preferences, storytelling, use of materials, and so on. This can be an entry as simple as "Blaine and Athena leading and directing play at big blocks—making large houses again," but it can also be an entry like "discussions of race and gender continue with dolls at the water table. Wonder what is needed to take discussions to another level." It can even begin with a mundane September entry like, "Faiza and Kedemah were dancing in the music corner while several others watched," which marked the beginning of the most sustained grassroots dialogue I've ever had (more on this in the next chapter).

However it begins, it always needs us to make the crucial response. For that there are no schedules, no formulas, and no fixed procedures to rely on. Responding to and building on an initiative—a delicate and intuitive piece of work—lies at the heart of teaching. The good news is that we generally get several chances to listen because like all of us, children will keep communicating until they are heard.

RECOMMENDED READING

Cambourne, Brian. *The Whole Story: Natural Learning and the Acquisition of Literacy in the Classroom.* Auckland, NZ: Ashton Scholastic, 1988.

This book offers an excellent outline of the structure of teaching literacy, which the author calls the "conditions of learning." I have found this framework especially useful in explaining all the aspects of teaching that go into generating understanding, but it could apply to any aspect of learning.

Cassidy, Diane, and Cathy Lancaster. "The Grassroots Curriculum: A Dialogue Between Children and Teachers." *Young Children,* 48 (1993): pp. 47–51.

This article discusses ways of planning and tracking a negotiated curriculum. I especially like its approach to tracking child-initiated and teacher-initiated directions over time. Worthwhile for those considering a more open-ended approach to curricula.

Gardner, Howard. *To Open Minds.* New York: Basic Books, 1989.

Gardner reports on his trip to China and his thinking about the role of structure in education, particularly arts education. As a "reflective practitioner," his is honest about having to rethink some of his positions.

Wasserman, Selma. *Serious Players in the Primary Classroom.* New York: Teachers College Press, 1990.

Wasserman, Selma, and J. W. George Ivany. *Teaching Elementary Science: Who's Afraid of Spiders?* Toronto: Harper and Row, 1988.

The play-debrief-replay model is set out in detail in these two books: in the first, outlined along with its applications for science, and in the second, part of a general discussion about structuring play.

Wells, Gordon, and Gen Ling Chang-Wells. *Constructing Knowledge Together: Classrooms as Centers of Inquiry and Literacy.* Portsmouth, NH: Heinemann, 1992.

An excellent book on the theory and practice of constructive inquiry. It, too, focuses on science, but emphasizes the ways in which children come to reason more abstractly about the world around them. The book's overall tone and approach follow on Vygotsky's theories of how children come to make meaning.

5

Passionate Learners

"Every class is different." It is easy for teachers to say this, but the reality gets up and bites, especially if the previous class seemed well suited to their temperament, pace, and ideals of what teaching and learning can be. I've struggled with my most recent class. Unlike the previous group of focused, purposeful learners, who knew exactly what they were going to do on any given day, this class didn't even seem to care about what day it was. It was a large group and so "*very* active," as many visitors remarked. The students seemed to be everywhere at once (and I swear some of them were). *Needy* is also a word that comes to mind, since there were many more fights, arguments, and demands for individual attention. The writing and drawing tables were almost empty on many days; it took much encouragement and modeling to get children to visit them.

Some of the early things I tried, such as storytelling and music performances, I did in response to the requests of the few remaining members of the previous class. It seemed that they too missed that class, and these activities represented much of what was strong about that group.

It was not all bad, of course. The children responded to a wide range of books, though they showed an early preference for alphabet books of all kinds that almost verged on hunger. The daily schedule was as popular as ever and worked well to provide a sense of organization. And there were other positive differences. I hardly had to teach some of the children to swing across the monkey bars, ride scooters, or throw balls. For others, learning to do these things well became a critical project. Large construction projects went up all the time and were never the same from day to day. The children closely analyzed pictures of previous building efforts for any usable ideas. One of the first times the class came together was in constructing a tunnel from old rubber tires. They cheered and congratulated classmates as they crawled through the tunnel, which was a real feat of coordination and risk taking. It was also apparent that they would try anything for a snack and eat a lot of it. They gobbled down fresh fruit, fresh vegetables, breads, cheeses, and crackers of all kinds without hesitation. It seems funny to say, but they were confident about eating.

I found myself scheduling gym times and outdoor large-muscle activity times back to back, and at the beginning of the afternoon instead of at the end. The rest of the day worked better that way. It might seem obvious that this class needed to move, but they needed so many other things as well—to learn to be members of a cooperative group, to learn to respect the personal space of others, and most of all to know, deep down, that they were really good at something.

Into this environment came Darcia Isenor, a university student on placement at our center. The presence of other adults in the classroom enriches the lives of the children, and I often seem to get people whose intelligences perfectly match their needs. This year was no exception: Darcia had a background in dance.

Even at that, it took me long enough to get around to suggesting that she consider doing some kind of dance lesson or demonstration for the class. When she began by showing simple hand, foot, and whole-body moves, it was like offering Einstein a math book. Alive, engaged, and immediately successful, many of the children danced and danced some more.

They suddenly really cared about what day it was—was Ms. Isenor coming today? Tomorrow?

"Why do you want to know?" I asked.

After a moment of quiet, one girl whispered, "We just like to dance, is all."

PASSIONS

Gardner wrote one of his more obscure musings about multiple intelligences soon after *Frames of Mind* appeared in 1983. It had to do with what was termed "crystallizing experiences" (Walters and Gardner 1984).

As defined by the authors, these were experiences that "involve remarkable and memorable contact between a person with unusual talent or potential and the materials of the field in which that talent will be manifested" (p. 6). Throughout the report, they tell anecdotes of famous artists, musicians, and scientists who recall the memorable moment when they knew they had found their calling. Watching Darcia Isenor with the children, I thought of these anecdotes. Perhaps some of them experienced such moments during the course of that dancing year—after Darcia's first dance demonstrations, or while watching a dance video, or when putting on tap shoes for the first time. From such moments come the passions that drive learning.

Passions are the result of children's intelligences at work. One of the greatest treats in teaching is discovering the passion of an individual or a whole class. The structure to construction cycle can begin. When their passions are unleashed, children are tremendously motivated to think. Passion can be infectious. Even the nondancers in the class loved to dance, and as their teacher, I found it easy to ride this enthusiasm to other places. We watched videos of many types of dance from around the world, listened to all kinds of music, tried on different styles of shoes, and explored ways of staging dance in the classroom.

We may not always like children's passions. It took me some time to appreciate children's need to move and I still found it important to make modifications to accommodate it. Letting go of the way you want to do things or have done them before can be hard.

All teachers have had the experience of accommodating (or fighting against) a class. The latest toys, television shows, or fads appear in our classrooms before we've even heard of them, let alone considered a response. One by one, these things do not constitute a passion, but if children keep showing up with the latest doll or comic, it is a sign that a passion of some kind is waiting to be released. Most passions can be directed in productive ways. In the case of toys, it may be that reading, writing, mathematics, or even myths and legends are associated (in later chapters, I'll give examples of how to use entry points to direct and respond to a passion).

Far from exploding into a classroom, however, many passions take time to develop, perhaps because we don't immediately recognize them or feed them. Children's passions often lurk quietly, waiting for an opportunity to come to life. It is worthwhile to observe who is watching, listening, and always nearby when a certain kind of activity is going on. In my class, there was always someone dancing to music in the beginning, but most children just watched out of the corner of their eye. Bit by bit, we began to offer activities, beginning with the larger dance of teaching. We arranged small group instruction and practice for those interested in an atrium space and large group activities in the gym once a week. Space was always available.

Children responded in a range of ways. Some held back and watched from the sidelines like wallflowers until they looked as if they were going to burst. Others plunged in fearlessly even if they had never danced before. The most minimal direction was enough to get them enthusiastically involved. One small group methodically sampled a dance activity in little bites and then returned to their previous activity. And a few needed guidance and instruction from Darcia Isenor in large and small group sessions before they became engaged.

In the end, all the children were intrigued by dance and movement. Their young age offered both possibilities and limitations in terms of how far we felt we could go with dance: possibilities because the children didn't have preconceived notions of who could and couldn't dance—boys would as happily clatter around the classroom in tap shoes as girls, and no form of dance was dismissed as inherently "uncool"—and limitations because the children could tolerate only short demonstrations due to their stamina. They had limited experience working as part of a group so any choreographed work was very simple. Through it all, Darcia and I constantly weighed how much structure and direction to give and grappled with whether or not to try to take some of the learning into a more formal performance. In the end, we created a community of learners who shared a passion and took off in ways we couldn't have envisioned.

COMMUNITIES OF LEARNERS: STUDENTS AS MENTORS

Gardner's background in arts education leads him to assume that between two (or more) people with a certain kind of intelligence, a kind of mediation happens when they have a specific focus for that intelligence (1993a). A painter can speak to another painter in a way that someone without that specialized knowledge cannot. This goes back to the idea that intelligences consist of symbols, not all of which are linguistic.

Students come to school with a wide variety of intelligences, which show themselves in many forms. They analyze, create, and apply knowledge. They have passionate interests that manifest themselves in the "real-world" applications they want to pursue. Every child is a unique mix, yet seeks a "partner" to dance with. The "partner" can be blocks, books, or instruments. It can be an open space for movement or a contained area for quiet huddling. The "partner" can also be the teacher, whose passion

Figure 5   Among the many places we danced was the gym. Here Joseph and Melanie are among the children improvising to different forms of movement.

for a subject and gift of just enough structure can help the novice feel successful.

Most often, though, the "partner" is a group. Such groups form in every classroom, and they are especially easy to spot in kindergarten. I have already discussed dancing, and indeed it involved a large group. However, there is always a group at the large block area, a group at computers, and another at the sand table or in the book corner. Sometimes the membership changes but usually not before the previous group members have somehow passed some of their knowledge on.

All intelligences, at different ages, seek communities that not only learn from each other but provide a subculture. Musicians hang around with other musicians, artists with other artists, dancers with other dancers. I suspect that people with strong reflective tendencies tend to search out others in book groups, self-help groups, and the like, and that people with strong bodily-kinesthetic intelligences tend to be the ones who want to go dancing or play sports. I would also guess that being immersed in a subculture extends children's knowledge of the metaphors, the attitudes, and the "technical" talk characteristic of every discipline.

When I finally realized this, I began to look around the classroom to discover and listen to the communities that existed there. In this year's class, for example, there were the computer kids, a reliable group who took pleasure in watching other children work on the computer, offering advice and answering questions for the less skilled. Having mastered a basic math and alphabet program, they then began to drift away, but not before teaching the next group how to use the program. The computer group often called on Jonathon for help with little crashes on the system. I was practically the last to know about Jonathon's rescue missions, in which he would turn off the system and completely reload everything. Who taught him to do that? I did, apparently, while he was hanging around watching me solve different problems.

Then there were the builders, a mixed group of boys and girls who made tunnels, bridges, and pirate ships—at least I knew who the leaders were, but I hadn't realized that one of the reasons they were leaders was that they were willing to be caught in an avalanche of blocks. This became clear when Blaine was called over to "test" a tunnel. He made some fixes that made it (a little) more stable and climbed in.

There were also the puzzle children, who liked to assemble puzzles as fast as they could, a large painting group that kept the paint tray full and the available wall space covered, and a water table group, who managed to immerse virtually every activity in the water table. This group built underwater tunnels with plastic blocks, used dolls in the water for storytelling, and colored the water to make paint. Literacy was a challenge until they found a plastic "Jack and the Beanstalk" book meant for infants, and lo and behold, even literacy was immersed.

To be sure, some children consistently seek solitude and quiet, and they too need classroom space. But listening in on the conversations of a community of learners presents a fascinating picture of what is important in nurturing a passion and reveals who is leading, who is learning, and just what kind of thinking is going on. At a certain point, the role of the teacher is simply to keep the little community of learners going with the tools and time they need to exercise their collective intelligence: a video here, a book there, time to watch a performance and offer feedback.

Over time, members of a community can start to have differing interpretations of what it means to be a member of the group. Some of the fiercest arguments about sports rules occur among the most sports minded; in some cases, they splinter the group into subgroups. Nothing so dramatic happened in our dance sessions, but there were continual variations on the theme. One day I walked into a group of children conducting an elaborate mock fight scene. No one was being hurt, but I expressed reservations. The group replied that they were just dancing! They compared some of their movements to those we were doing in the dance sessions. Imagine, aesthetics and rationalization all in one move. About two weeks later, the scenario shifted. This time there was an elaborate fight scene, but only one person was orchestrating the play, while the others responded to the directions. This time, they said they were "dancing a video game." That phrase became a spur to some of the other children. They made their own video show, based on dance shows they had seen on television. They constructed a stage, selected an announcer, and performed.

The community was alive and well.

FLOW

One of the challenges I give myself is to create a thinking program that appeals to all, but it is not always easy. I have certainly met and taught children with little intrinsic motivation, who simply waited for the next direction or consequence. Such learners are entirely dependent on adults, not only for learning but for the *pleasure* of learning. Yet students need to experience the pleasure of learning and practicing learning for its own sake, with no other audience than themselves. We all want our learners to develop such intrinsic motivation. For me, the best explanation of where such motivation comes from is the work of Mihalyi Csikszentmihalyi (1990, 1996), who describes a powerful internal state of consciousness he calls "flow." In this state of deep engagement, learners are so in tune with what is happening, they become unaware of events around them. Time works to their advantage, seeming either to slow down or speed up as necessary. It is a moment of high creativity.

For Gardner (1993b), this "flow" state is intrinsically rewarding. In his view, once learners have experienced it, they will want to experience it again. This explains why people return to a difficult activity. What was dull routine, practiced over and over, becomes "flow": the repetition of the task is suddenly a pleasure. A writer gets to a place where words and ideas fly together, a painter begins to paint in a novel style, an athlete completes a difficult maneuver with ease.

Here I want to return to the deeper value of structure. Routines organize attention and effort by making skills automatic, freeing attention for the more difficult tasks at hand. Mastering brush strokes, for example, allows children to concentrate on where they will apply them. True, this kind of easy effort takes practice. The teacher's job is often simply to help structure the practice until learners can take over for themselves.

Once children experience a certain amount of success at discipline and get into the "rhythm" of it, they are more likely to return to it on their own. Structure encourages the development of intrinsic motivation. Like riding a bicycle or learning to drive a car, once the basics are mastered, the learner wants to keep going in order to get to new and more exciting places. The job of a mediator is to maintain the energy, the focus, and the level of success a learner needs to master these routines. When a community of learners is involved, the level of "flow" becomes easier to achieve because the energy is maintained by the community.

"Flow" is not simply a state when practiced skills come together. It is a state in which challenges seem to add spice to activity and increase the state of engagement and enjoyment. Something as simple as a deadline can be such a challenge. Many people I know experience marvelous bursts of creativity as a deadline nears. A teacher's well-timed challenge to add to a painting or a construction can also produce such learning. Mastering a new technique and having it become part of an overall repertoire is another such example of a challenge that can produce this state of blissful absorption.

All teachers have experienced moments of flow as teachers—days when it all comes together, the routines are seamless, the students engaged and everything works. I have been lucky enough to have been in classrooms when the whole dance flows along seamlessly and with complexity. The bell rings before anyone knows it. It is worth remembering what it takes to get to such moments, all the repetition, the negotiation, and the scaffolding of new ideas and practices. At the moment of maximum "flow," who would want someone to interrupt or to have to go to an assembly in the gym or to have an administrator come in to ask for a forgotten piece of paper?

The "flow" moment should be respected and left uninterrupted if we truly want our children to enjoy learning and develop into independent learners. Throughout this book, I emphasize *time,* which is a critical ingredient in a thinking classroom. As teachers, we can't always predict how much time we'll need or when, but we should be aware of how destructive an interruption can be to this dynamic involvement.

The classroom dance goes on. It has become an inherent part of who these children are and what they do. They have discovered how to learn about animals through dance, stories through movement, and science through action. The days, weeks, and months flow on.

———

It all sounds too easy, and I can hear some readers wondering how they could justify pursuing certain subjects further instead of covering the curricula. Teachers may want to do this kind of intensive work but face strict mandates and pressure to conform. I have no easy answer, but it may be worth considering Gardner's suggested "personalization" of education. He does not think it critical that people know about and use the theory of multiple intelligences. What is more important is that "differences among youngsters are taken seriously, knowledge about differences is shared with children and parents, children gradually assume responsibility for their own learning, and materials that are worth knowing are presented in ways that afford each child the maximum opportunity to master those materials and to show others (and themselves) what they have learned and understood" (1995, p. 209).

If all schools were run (and funded) according to such a vision, I wonder what the result would be? I would like to think that schools would be happier, more humane, and more productive places for children and teachers.

RECOMMENDED READING

Donaldson, Margaret. *Human Minds: An Exploration.* Toronto: Penguin Books, 1993.
> This is one of my favorite books about cognition because it takes into account not only cognitive but emotional and spiritual development. It is also important because it attempts to synthesize Western and Eastern perspectives into a unique framework for understanding cognitive development.

Morgan, Norah, and Julianna Saxton. *Asking Better Questions: Models, Techniques and Classroom Activities for Engaging Students in Learning.* Markham, ON: Pembroke Publishers, 1994.

This is a fine resource for developing specific skills in questioning. The authors articulate the ways in which different teachers' questions promote refined student understanding. They also outline stategies for fostering better student questions.

Wood, David. *How Children Think and Learn.* Cambridge, MA: Basil Blackwell, 1988.

A good introduction to some of the issues involved in the development of children's cognition. It covers both Piaget and Vygotsky and ranges from reading to math. Although it does not discuss multiple intelligences directly, I have found it to be a useful reference for basic language and literacy concepts.

6

Intelligent Assessment

It was Halloween in kindergarten, a time for masks, mystery, and morbid fascinations. In my program, I do not give Halloween much attention, since it seems to do just fine on the children's own initiative. However, we had been to the pumpkin farm to select pumpkins for home and for the classroom. The kids carved the pumpkins and placed them around the room. One location was by the snack table. One day Paulo was alone at the table quietly eating and apparently talking to himself. He'd done this before, but I hadn't wanted to ask what he was doing lest I interrupt him. Still, there are moments in a classroom when you just *have* to know what is going on right then and there, and this was such a moment for me.

I asked Paulo whom he was talking to. "The pumpkin," he replied with one of those "isn't that obvious" looks young children give to uninformed teachers like me.

"Oh, yes," I said. "What are you talking to the pumpkin about today?" I used my best, "been meaning to talk with the pumpkins myself" tone of voice to invite his response.

"Well," Paulo replied, "he wants to talk to his friend over there [a pumpkin on the other side of the class] because he's lonely."

Paulo and I continued to chat for another minute or so about solutions to this pumpkin problem. Paulo was of the view that simply reorienting the pumpkins so that they could see one another was the way to proceed. He had checked this out with the pumpkin and that solution was okay with it. I gave my blessing to the plan. I was almost ready to walk away with that "another problem solved" feeling, when Paulo looked up at me and began to whisper out of the side of his mouth, presumably so the pumpkin couldn't hear.

"The pumpkin doesn't really talk," he said. "I'm just using my demagination."

"Demagination?"

"Yeah," he said, "my demagination. It's invisible from my brain."

───────

Assessing Paulo's imagination is not a simple case of observing his behavior. It is an interactive process of move and countermove, an endless series of dances. Even if I am simply the audience, I am still influencing the performance. What is in the classroom and what is not, what is on the agenda for the class and what is not, can all affect children's learning and thinking. How do I assess thinking in all its forms?

Discussions about what thinking is and how best to measure it are fraught with difficulty. Unable to "see" cognition directly, we grope and guess our way through bits of evidence. Sometimes we find something tangible and sometimes we find the evidence to be far less clear. If only I could hold a child's thinking still at one time and in one place with no distractions and measure it—but assessment really doesn't work that way.

So the question becomes how best to assess Paulo's intelligence? And how can he be involved in the assessment process, since he already knows so much about his own thinking? How can he be assessed in a way that is fair and that he can understand?

ASSESSMENT AND MULTIPLE INTELLIGENCES

There have been a number of attempts to use a multiple intelligence framework to assess thinking. Checklists, such as the one devised by Thomas Armstrong (1994), are easy for teachers but limited in what they look at. In addition, they divide a child's performance into seven (or eight) neat intelligences, which is an artificial way of looking at thinking.

More noteworthy in my opinion is the work of Mara Krechevsky (1994) and the Project Spectrum group reported in *Project Spectrum: Preschool Assessment Handbook.* This book covers a wide range of variables relating to the intelligences and includes assessment protocols and recording charts for tasks related to each intelligence. The approach outlined in this book, however, presents two problems. First, having a single activity for each intelligence is a limiting factor in a regular classroom, where a wide range of activities occur. It is difficult to isolate and focus on a single task for a single child. Second, attempting to define an intelligence through a single task is practically impossible. Any human activity involves any number of symbol systems.

Over the last few years, Gardner has discussed ways in which the intelligences might be appropriately assessed. His own position on what constitutes good assessment practice has evolved: I can remember reading reports ten years ago that he was working on specific tests of intelligences. (Indeed, the *Project Spectrum Preschool Assessment Handbook* was one result of this experimentation.)

Over time, however, he has moved to the position that thinking cannot be directly assessed: "Despite the seductive terminology, we cannot assess the intelligences: We can at most assess proficiency in different tasks" (1996, p. 4). Thus, while he might note how well someone learned and transformed a song as an important piece of evidence, he would caution that this might not be evidence of a purely musical intelligence at work but of an entirely different one.

These statements may appear to complicate the assessment process, but they are realistic. Children do not have to be pigeonholed. Gardner is not breaking away from his previous position but holding to his belief that assessment should be as "intelligence fair" as possible. "Intelligence-fair" classroom environments, teaching, and assessment are the core of any assessment framework (Gardner 1991, 1995). These classrooms offer a range of possible products and performances, from dance to decimals, from reading to reflecting. Children learn, represent, and reflect on their learning in unique ways.

A PORTFOLIO FRAMEWORK

According to Gardner, the purpose of assessment is to generate information useful in planning activities that challenge and extend the ways individuals manifest their intelligences. Gardner has nominated the portfolio as one way such assessment can take place. Children select examples of their work for a portfolio over a term or a year. It becomes a record of their growth. The very act of selecting their best work and deciding why it is their best work or what they might have done differently gives them a share in the responsibility for evaluation. Gardner considers portfolio-based assessment as a primary method of "intelligence-fair" assessment. From his point of view, portfolios represent a more accurate record of children's performance.

The longer I work with portfolios, the more I agree. Over the last few years, as I have found myself trying, with the assistance of many other teachers, to explain how to get children to see themselves as learners, the portfolio has offered the best answer.

The process of portfolio-based assessment rests on a basic framework: *collect, select, reflect,* and *project* (Burke, Fogarty, and Belgrad 1994). This four-stage framework has led to some of the best ways of assessing children in general. In my own case, it is easy to remember, it keeps me focused on a range of authentic assessment issues, and it yields a range of insights into what a learner may be thinking. Even those who don't use portfolios (and don't plan to) will discover a great deal to consider in their teaching and in assessing self-reflection.

Collecting

The other day I watched one of the children in my colleague Carol's morning kindergarten class prepare to go home. She held a plastic bag, and in it she put a painting she had done. Then she remembered that she had written a story, so she found that too. At the end of the morning, on her way back to the childcare space for lunch, she stopped to look at a picture of herself busily putting together a puzzle. She asked if she could have it, and as she added the photo to the contents of her bag, she listened to a piece of music and talked about how much she liked it. This child was collecting intelligences—artwork, organization, puzzles, writing, music, and social talk all wrapped in a personal perspective. If she had watered a plant on her way, she would have exercised every symbol system.

It isn't easy to collect evidence of different intelligences, and I am always wondering how to do it better. I use various methods but always wish I could think of more. For example, some of the things children make and do don't fit into a portfolio. Photographs help in those areas that are difficult to track, and they are compact and easy to store, but it can be hard to take photographs in enough settings to represent certain types of performances, like dance, fully. A good tape or video recording system in every corner of the room would be ideal, but I usually have to make do with occasional tapings.

When I do see a piece of work I like, children often want to take it home. Making a photocopy is a partial solution, but I wonder if children regard the copy as their "best work" when it is time to make selections. Going the other way, I think some children select the photocopy *because* something "magical" happened when it was copied.

And where does all this material get stored? I opt for a two-stage process: first in a large storage portfolio and later, during the selection stage, in a smaller, more compact portfolio. I have read of schools that store children's performances and work products on laser disk, and this may be the future but it isn't my present. In spite of the technical difficulties, children produce work and I collect some of it. It's not really hard to do in a classroom where we're like fish swimming in an ocean of work.

When he was four, Paulo began to use small tiles to make floors for block houses other children built. He would concentrate on the exact configurations of these floors for long periods of time. He also liked jigsaw puzzles and was often the first to start one when it came in. To be sure, he also enjoyed books, played with imagination and creativity, and loved to run— all the usual kindergarten things. What caught the eye, however, were these elaborate constructions.

At five, he began to draw. The drawings were his attempts to represent objects in three dimensions or to represent detailed and intricate designs. He also began to experiment with complicated three-dimensional creations made of tubes, boxes, and other leftover bits. On a day when I told him he had to do something besides box gluing, he sat in front of the box gluing corner and drew a detailed picture of people working at box gluing (who says five-year-olds haven't got a subtle sense of humor?).

One day Paulo walked into class and announced that he had a song to sing. At the end of the day, I made time for him to do this and he proceeded to half tell and half sing a long story, complete with a refrain: "He went up, up, up, up and then he went down, down, down, down," during which he accompanied himself by going up and down the notes on the piano. I asked him where he got the idea and he said it came from a tape he had at home. He also affirmed that he had a piano.

His performance was a big hit in the kindergarten classroom and sparked a run of other songs, stories, and plays. I had to change the schedule to accommodate the demand. Although I have only anecdotal notes and a few pictures of this event, it seems enough for Paulo to recall it a year after the

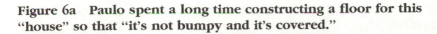

Figure 6a   Paulo spent a long time constructing a floor for this "house" so that "it's not bumpy and it's covered."

fact. He remembers the song he sang that day better than I do. Still, it is one of those things that has made me resolve to teach the children to audiotape themselves, a work-in-progress.

When I got around to mentioning to his mother that he was playing the piano at school, she blinked in surprise. She said he had never played the piano at home and the tapes he was referring to were stories but had no music on them. So where did he get the idea?

"My brain," Paulo said. "I just thought it."

Like any child given the opportunity, Paulo creates a lot of work worth collecting. The next issue is probably the most critical: how to select from this large body of work?

Figure 6b   Paulo's picture of box gluing. It was drawn from a ground perspective, which is "how come you can see the feet."

Selecting

One day, Paulo was lying on the floor feigning unconsciousness, one of those fads that ripple through the kindergarten from time to time. It had been sparked by a book, *Now, Now Markus* (Auer and Klages 1988) in which Markus "drops dead" until he gets a bird. In this case, however, Paulo was lying on the floor at the start of activity time, an hour-long period of free choice during which children are expected to direct themselves. When I finally got around to asking him his reason for "fainting," he replied, "My brain got tired trying to decide what to do."

For children, one of the most important aspects of learning to select their best work is first learning to make choices. Young children today have choices in a lot of areas—what clothes to wear, what food to eat, what activity they want to do. Making decisions in these areas lays the groundwork for selecting work for their portfolio. When a child makes a choice, the adult can reflect back with them on the choices they have made before ("You really are doing a lot of thinking at the big blocks") or emphasize new ones ("Hey, that's the first time you've chosen computer"). Each choice is a step toward understanding that one of their roles as learners is to choose. This may sound simple, but if a child has no practice in making choices, then when it comes time to select a piece of work for the portfolio, they are more likely to shrug and let the adult choose for them.

I once watched an exchange between a teacher and an eight-year-old boy about which piece of his work he wanted to put into a display case. The boy hemmed and hawed, tried the counting out rhyme, eeny, meeny, miny, mo, but finally couldn't decide. Apparently, the discussion had gone on for days. Finally, in exasperation, the teacher said, "Oh just pick one you think your mother would like!" The boy looked up with one of those "why didn't you say so" looks and immediately selected a symmetrical drawing. "She likes flowers," he said. "She'll like this."

A key factor in learning to select is the idea of *audience*. Even young children make distinctions between work their younger sibling might like, work their mother might like, and work they like themselves. The teacher just has to ask the right question in the right way. One of the little things I learned from that eight-year-old was the importance of understanding who the audience is, either explicitly or implicitly. Consider asking a question like "Where does this work go—in a portfolio so you can look at it in the future, on the classroom wall so you can look at it now, or home so your parents can see it?" It is not surprising that children often choose their parents, because their parents are their first audience and they want them to see everything. However, it is worth staying with such questions. I feel it is a sign of progress when a child begins to select work for the classroom wall: it indicates that the audience has expanded to include the teacher and classmates instead of just a "home" audience.

One of the basic reasons for portfolios, display cases, walls, and bulletin boards is to encourage children to expand their sense of audience. The issue is more than pleasing someone else: it is about getting children to think about aesthetics. After all, different audiences have different tastes, and children often understand this; the eight-year-old knew his mother liked flowers.

Learning to pick your best work is not easy. Children should start before they become so self-conscious they can't manage the challenge. Here again a multiple intelligences framework is helpful. I have discussed Gardner's eight intelligences with children to illustrate different kinds of "smart," because they are reasonably easy to explain and visually easy to represent. Of course, I *do not* force children to stay within this framework; it simply gives them language for talking about their thinking. This language becomes another set of criteria for use in making selections. Telling a child to choose one "picture smart" product (a good drawing, painting, or design) for a portfolio is concrete enough for even a young child. Similarly, terms like "body smart," "people smart," and the like are helpful starting points (Armstrong 1994). Gardner's intelligences also give them a way to talk about what they're good at. They begin to see the connection between their work and the work of their brain. Once children can talk about different *kinds* of smarts, they move on to which *domains* they are smart in. They begin to report that they are "computer smart," "gym smart," "dancing smart," and so on. Not only does this help them in selecting work, it also helps them to see themselves as participants in these domains and to develop a sense of reflection.

Paulo reacted to the portfolio with the typical kindergarten approach. He ignored it except when I asked him directly to put in some material. He did like to have his photograph taken and would take home work he was excited about. He also liked to put his work up around the classroom and would point to a piece with pride if a visitor asked about it.

One day this past fall, I made a special fuss over one of his drawings and strongly suggested he include it in his portfolio. He didn't want to but instead suggested putting it up on the wall. He spent several minutes pondering, wandering around the room, and lamenting that all the good places were taken. Finally, he located a suitable place and put it up. I considered his fussiness a good sign because he was searching for just the right place for his creation. It was an indicator that selecting work was coming.

Yet I could not have predicted what happened later in the fall. One day Paulo ran into the classroom and announced that he had to, just had to, go to the writing table immediately. There was an idea "in his brain" that he had to "get out" immediately.

At the writing table he selected a very large piece of paper. Carefully choosing a marker, he drew a very small square. "There," he said. "I made a square."

"Great," I replied uncertainly. "Is that your idea—a small square on a large piece of paper?"

He looked at me and told me he was thinking.

Figure 6c   Turning a square into a diamond "before my brain forgets how to make it."

He then drew a diamond shape on the page. "*This* is my idea," he said. "When you turn a square, it looks like a diamond." (And where had he gotten this idea? "By watching the men make driveways," he replied. "You know, the stones they use.")

More important than this discovery was what he said, "This should go in my portfolio!" Paulo was beginning to select work, recognize its quality, and make a reflective comment right on the spot. Moreover, he had begun to understand that the portfolio was more than a storage place. He was beginning to assess himself and helping me to do so as well. As children produce a greater range of work—drawings, stories, paintings, math work—they have more to select from for their portfolio. Eventually a teacher asks for a best drawing, a best piece of handwriting, a best story for the portfolio.

Reflecting

Producing and selecting items for the portfolio are large steps on the way to reflection. As different work is produced, it becomes easier for children to see, hear, and feel many ways of knowing. Our class discussions of various ways of being smart emphasize the idea that thinking is our primary goal. Reflection is the cornerstone of any thinking program. Without it, children would not perceive themselves as learners. There are a number of ways to improve reflection and some of them are discussed in the chapters ahead. However, children need another piece in order to be able to reflect. An increasingly fascinating area of research (for example, Astington 1993; Wellman 1990) called theory of mind suggests that even young children become aware not only of their own thinking but of the whole notion of cognition in general. The more aware of what and how they think learners are, the more confident they will be in going ahead by themselves.

Carol, my teaching partner, and I talk about the brain often in our prospective kindergarten programs. The classroom has models of the brain children can touch and posters of the brain they can look at. Of all the parts of the body, children should know about the brain. Most young children can learn this, and once they do, they begin to connect healthy living (taking care of your brain), portfolios (an extension of your brain), and "brain language." They learn to think of learning as a system.

By "brain language," I mean the cognitive verbs we use all the time—words like *think, imagine, guess, wonder,* and *plan*—and assume learners will pick up. I try to use this kind of language with great deliberateness when I speak or when I read a story with works like these. It is most important that children acquire this vocabulary.

Children's concepts of time are another key element in helping them understand the process of looking back. Recently, a teacher told me that she used her students' baby pictures to introduce them to the process of looking back at their learning. It was another one of those obvious ideas that never quite occurred to me. Reflection is easier the farther back we look. This is true for all of us, and realizing it is a great help. It allows us to begin to teach children how to see the changes in their lives brought about through learning. Learning to walk, learning to talk, learning to ride a trike, learning to put on your coat are all simple accomplishments that children can understand as learning.

The principle of looking back has also helped me in my portfolio interviews with children. The earlier the work they look at, the more they begin to see and articulate the changes. This kind of comparison also sets up a framework for children to search for smaller changes among their more recent work.

It should be obvious even to those who don't know him that Paulo has acquired the language of thinking. He is a prime example of a learner with a natural facility for self-reflection interacting with an environment in which the symbols of reflection were constantly being demonstrated. Not all our learners become this fluent in using cognitive words, but all leave kindergarten with the basic vocabulary.

A sense of time is important in teaching any child to reflect back on his or her work. In Paulo's case, this was confirmed in an interview at the time he put the square-to-diamond drawing into his portfolio. It was as if, by putting the work in the portfolio himself, he noticed it for the first time. He began sorting through other pieces of work. He stopped to look at the picture of a dragon he had made and said, "Hey remember that? . . . those are like things from my last year's brain!" His comment is significant, but even more important is his understanding of the process of cognitive growth. In his own eyes, Paulo was a learner.

Projecting

My colleague Sue Loban runs a middle school program based on independent work skills, group work, and developing true thinking. As part of her evaluation process, her students take part in interviews with outside evaluators to talk about their explicit understanding of the relationship between the curriculum and talk about their own work. I had the chance to be a member of the team interviewing an eighth-grade student.

The student had selected examples of his work from different areas of the curriculum and in response to prompts—the work you were proudest of, the work that improved the most, and so on. Among the pieces this young man had selected was a short writing project on black history. He had interviewed family members for their recollections and family stories (relatives had been slaves) and carried out his own research. It was a nice piece of work, and the student obviously had a passion for the subject.

I asked where he would go next with this project if he had the chance. I expected him to say he would investigate a certain era further or research a certain figure in more detail. But the question caught him by surprise, and he spent a long minute thinking before he replied. "I guess I'd like to find out how come some people think they are better than others. I would want to know when that happened." This student obviously knows how to project ahead.

The concepts of time and brain talk are also helpful in teaching projecting, which requires a what-would-you-do-next-time sense of the future. When children have older siblings, I sometimes start by asking what they might do differently when they are as old as their sibling. This gets some children commenting on how their work might change in the future, but many have said that they'd be neater or a better speller, as if the technical and mechanical aspects of performance are the most concrete changes they can imagine.

Projecting also requires understanding another set of words and phrases—*what if, plan,* and *same and different*—and seeing that one part can be changed without harming the whole. This is very hard for young children to do. It requires a sense of the aesthetics of a subject, the appropriate vocabulary, and a desire to change what is already done, which can also be enormously difficult for any of us.

However, one of the ways to teach young children how to project ahead is to get them together as a group to brainstorm ways to change something that I, or another adult, has done. I might, for example, tell a story while illustrating it on the chalkboard and then invite the class to make changes. (Reading a story aloud does not have the same effect, since, like many adults, children consider the written word more immune to change.) "What should I tell the next time?" I'll ask.

I don't want to imply, however, that it is impossible to get children who are full of confidence to at least consider some kind of change to their own work. Not long ago, I pulled out the squares to diamonds drawing from Paulo's portfolio and challenged him to come up with other examples of rotations.

Paulo considered this for a minute and said, "I can't."

"Why not?"

"Well, because the men don't make a driveway until the summer. It's not summer. I can't get new ideas until next summer."

It may not seem at first that Paulo answered the challenge to demonstrate other rotations in space, but he did have a plan and was using words like *next* and *until.* He was clearly moving ahead.

It was in the realm of storytelling that Paulo really began to demonstrate a strong ability to project ahead. When I told a story about a girl looking for buried treasure, I had her decide to give some of the treasure back to the dragon that had helped her. This was too much for Paulo, who had kept up a running commentary. In *his* story, he said, the dragon would just do the right thing for no reward. Who knows where this vibrant child will go next?

REFLECTIONS—AND PROJECTIONS

As information about a child starts to roll in from different sources, we start to see patterns. At this point it can be tempting to conclude that a child has more of one kind of intelligence or ability than another. Here, it is wise to be careful lest these expectations become a self-fulfilling prophecy. I can remember one case in which someone thought a child was supposed to be autistic and managed to identify autistic behaviors everywhere, only to find out that the child under observation was not diagnosed with autism. At the same time, regularities in a child's performance over time can indicate that they focus more on some areas than on others. In any balanced assessment, we need to remember that most children demonstrate many intelligences over time.

The Paulo anecdotes I've told occurred over a period of about a year. In that time, he was making products that demonstrated some of the ways he liked to think and his obvious attraction to activities with a strong visual and spatial component. He also liked to create and apply his knowledge, but his time out of school obviously went to analyzing how others configured materials. To call him a "visual-spatial" learner, however, does not do him justice. He is also very thoughtful, imaginative, and creative, with an extraordinary power of concentration. These are intrapersonal qualities. During this same time, he was reading many pattern books, becoming more coordinated, making friends, and learning to run programs on the computer.

To find out what I have learned about a child, I make predictions to myself. In Paulo's case, I predicted that he would, in the immediate future, be intrigued by new puzzles, display an aptitude for units on visual patterning, eagerly participate in activities having to do with measurement, and probably enjoy books about shapes and images. These predictions have, for the most part, been true. Paulo continues to be engaged by anything with strong visual-spatial and numerical components. It seems fair to credit him with analytical, creative, and practical intelligence. Visual and spatial symbols strongly attract him, and he has consistently demonstrated his capacity to use them. Yet one cannot ignore the thoughtful reflection, concentration, and persistence he brings to many tasks. Beyond this, it is clear that he can make connections between diverse pieces. He even has a sense of how to perform for an audience.

This hardly means he won't pursue other skills and other forms of knowing. It seems reasonable to assume, however, that the inner drive will always be there somewhere and the fascination with the visual and spatial never far away.

Paulo is one learner. Other learners would have very different profiles and present different problems for those tracking and recording their intelligences. Learners with significant academic difficulties might rely more heavily on our assistance to produce any work. They might also require more careful day-to-day tracking for small indications of intelligence at work. Still other children might only produce certain types of work and never venture far from that strength.

Even with an overview of a class or an individual, we still need to plan how we will approach the curriculum. It is here that the entry points become useful. Whatever a learner's strengths, there are ways to use one or more of them in building knowledge.

RECOMMENDED READING

Armstrong, Thomas. *Multiple Intelligences in the Classroom,* Alexandria, VA: Association for Supervision and Curriculum Development, 1994.

A highly accessible book about applying multiple intelligence theory to classrooms. It can seem a little simplistic at times, but I know many teachers who consider it the best book on the subject.

Krechevsky, Mara. *Project Spectrum: Preschool Assessment Handbook.* Cambridge, MA: President and Fellows of Harvard College, 1994.

A detailed resource on assessment of the intelligences. Some of the strategies are too cumbersome to be used by regular classroom teachers but the ideas about what sorts of variables to consider in assessment are worthwhile.

Tierney, Robert J., Mark A. Carter, and Laura E. Desai. *Portfolio Assessment in the Reading-Writing Classroom.* Norwood, MA: Christopher Gordon, 1991.

A solid resource on the range of issues involved in portfolio-based assessment. The focus is literacy portfolios, but the authors cover a range of bases, including some of the Arts Propel research. There is also an excellent review of some of the literature around authentic assessment.

Part II

Teaching with Gardner's Entry Points and Thinking About Their Implications

7

Intelligent Questions: Philosophy

Some time after Aisha and I had our discussion on questions ("you want me to ask questions every single day?!" See Chapter 1), on a particularly hectic day in class, she raised her hand. "I gotta question to ask." I asked what the question was, but the look on her face suggested that this was not going to be so simple.

"I gotta question to ask and I bet you don't even know what I'm gonna ask! You might *think* you know what I'm gonna ask, but you don't *really* know. You'd like to know 'cause it's a good question and I've been thinking about it. I talked to my friends about it. I've even dreamed about asking it," she said. "Wouldn't you like to see in my brain to find out without my askin'? Then it would be so easy for you!"

This back and forth continued for another minute, long enough, I assume, for her to get the attention of the rest of the class. Finally, I gave her one of those looks that said "enough." She asked, "Where do questions come from? How come you can't see them? Why don't they have a computer and you could just ask and it would tell you the answer to stuff you wanna know? Then nobody would ever need to go to school!"

I deferred the issue to later in the day. It occurred to me that its *timing* had much to do with the fact that it was time for math, but these were, in their own way, a wonderful set of questions. Aisha touched on the nature of thinking, opened up a discussion of dreams, and brought up an idea with profound philosophical implications. She had clearly been thinking.

_I_nviting children to reflect on their own work is an important component of learning. It is a particular boon to those children who look inward. While this is critical, it is not enough to sustain learners who have intrapersonal strengths.

The entry point of philosophy draws heavily on linguistic abilities but is meant to accommodate more inwardly focused learners as they approach a variety of topics. It is important to understand at the outset that for this entry point Howard Gardner has in mind deep, philosophical kinds of questions: How come some people think they are better than others? and Where do questions come from? and Is there a God? Such fundamental questions are inherent in work about people and places, objects and events. They may be about ethical dilemmas, meditations about the origins of an idea, or speculation about the nature of thought and reality. This entry point draws heavily on intrapersonal symbols as well as language. Its social dimensions may not be directly apparent, but every time there is a classroom discussion of fairness or a question or right and wrong—which is a great deal of the time—the issues are social.

There is growing evidence that children do indeed think about fundamental questions. Robert Coles, for example (1986a, 1986b), has ably documented the ways in which children examine moral and spiritual questions. Aidan Chambers has made a career of getting children to ask and answer complex questions about the nature of literature. The next chapter considers researchers who find children thinking about thinking.

BUILDING PHILOSOPHICAL INQUIRY

Starting with Questions

Any philosophy program—in fact, any program that includes thinking—begins with questions. If children do not listen to teachers ask questions or ask their own questions, then the more complex, philosophical ones will probably not arise. Questions do not necessarily need an answer, but they do need an audience. Listening to a question, acknowledging a question, or eliciting one from a learner, validates it. Listening affirms the identity of the learner *as* a learner, as one who inquires. It also affirms and nurtures the learner's curiosity. It affirms that they have a thinking "brain."

I've come to believe that asking questions is not entirely a linguistic process; bringing a question to life is a practiced skill. This fits with the notion of multiple intelligences, but it has taken me a while to fully see it. Consider an infant with a caregiver. The infant registers surprise by a startle response, a widening of the eyes; it registers interest by tracking, by becoming still to listen, by reaching for an object. Then the caregiver, her intonation rising, says something like "What's that?" or "Who's that?" or "Where did it go?" or "What happened?" often physically supporting or mimicking the infant at the same time. In this moment, and many others like it, the infant learns about questions. It begins to anticipate, to take on the script of its caregiver, and to internalize the question as a linguistic form. In this context, the infant also experiences questions as a good thing; it attends to the novel and the surprising from a secure position.

As teachers, we often have moments of disequilibrium, but these are the moments that generate questions. Children perplex us, lessons go awry, and we feel that initial moment of bafflement. We might immediately ask ourselves what happened, or we come to feel that all is not right. That initial feeling is not a linguistic moment.

The child who stands back from a drawing and hesitates for a second before taking the next step, or the child trying to throw a ball a greater distance who looks at his hands and shifts his feet, but sees the ball land only two meters away—both are experiencing moments of wonder, surprise, or consternation, that internal feeling of a question.

Each intelligence must generate its own moment of surprise or wonder. I can remember showing a nonverbal but very visually oriented learner in my kindergarten a spinning disk that changed color and design as it spun. The child reacted with an almost painful startle when he first saw the disk and turned his head away. Later he approached it, slowly but with caution, occasionally checking with a nearby adult. We taught him to spell *disk*, and he stopped and respelled it a few times.

Was I sure he had a question? No, but I assumed that the moment of surprise indicated What's that? The fact that he continued to look reflected his interest. I suspect that many questions never make it into words. It's easier for teachers if they do, to be sure, but if we look for the moment of surprise, we will probably know where the questions are.

Philosophical Questions

If all this isn't enough, asking philosophical questions can be even more frustrating because one question leads to another and there seem to be no answers. Philosophical questions tend to be so fundamental, it is hard to know where to begin. They often arrive unannounced, out of the blue. The first task is therefore to identify ways of making such inquiry a little more predictable.

Philosophy has no tangible set of materials or tools to call its own. While this makes it very "portable"—usable in even the most underfunded school setting—it also makes it open-ended. Fortunately, several writers have provided teachers with some starting places. As part of his ongoing project on thinking in children, Matthew Lipman (1991) has developed an approach based on exploring philosophy. Similarly, Gareth Matthews (1984, 1994) has also written extensively on doing philosophy with children five and older. Both contribute to an excellent journal called simply *Thinking,* which is worth tracking down for its examples of philosophical inquiry with children. I have been fascinated by their ability to unearth philosophy in everything from art to children's literature.

Matthews has put together a formal commercial program called Philosophy for Children, which includes small novels and guided activities to start teachers off in philosophical reasoning. I have seen some of these materials and thought them worthwhile, but I do not, at this point, use them with my classes.

For both, the key components to facilitating philosophy are time, catalysts such as stories or questions, openness, and a belief in the value of such inquiry. They agree that philosophy is about dialogue—conversations that capture a spirit of inquiry.

A FRAMEWORK FOR INQUIRY AND DIALOGUE

We all like simple little frameworks we can use to cue and organize our teaching, and I am no exception. By far the best frame for inquiry and reflection I have discovered is one I learned almost by serendipity. It was meant to facilitate uncovering meaning in stories, but it has many applications. One of them is philosophy.

While working as a speech-language pathologist in a children's treatment center, I found myself at a workshop given by Aidan Chambers. Even now, I remember almost every moment of that workshop as if it were yesterday. It was one of those curious experiences when time goes so slowly that everything is clear, what Mihalyi Csikszentmihalyi might call a moment of "flow."

Chambers was outlining his "Tell Me" approach, a system for responding to reading, further elaborated in *Tell Me: Children, Reading, and Talk* (1996). It is his belief that even very young children can become knowledgeable critics of any book. In the process of doing so they become more aware, more responsible readers. Chambers claims that even children who haven't read the book or who can't read can make valuable contributions.

He had chosen *Grandpa,* a picture book by John Burningham, and invited people in the audience to read it through. He then made four columns, one marked "Likes," another "Dislikes," a third "Puzzles," and the final one "Patterns." He invited the audience to start with Likes by commenting on things they liked about the book, anything at all, for as he said then (and has repeated often since), all ideas are to be taken as honorably reported. People commented on liking pictures, words or phrases, and certain parts of the story. He did the same thing with Dislikes. Sometimes what one person liked another disliked. I remember that more than one person commented on not liking the ending of the book.

He then moved on to Puzzles, which he framed as anything that inspired a question or a sense of curiosity. In *Grandpa* there are many ambiguous pictures and lines of text. Indeed, one person said that she didn't care for the ambiguity of the book. This comment was added to the Dislikes pile. Parts of the text are printed in different fonts, the pictures use color in different ways, and words and pictures interrelate in unexpected ways. These features were puzzling. One person wondered about the different print fonts, another about what happened at the end of the book.

The final category, Patterns, involved ideas, words, or pictures that recurred throughout the text. People noticed obvious features, such as the repetition of the word *Grandpa,* as well as the less obvious, such as the sections of sepia-colored text.

I probably learned more about reading a book that day than ever before. I realized how much children could really say when asked or prompted in the right way. Because of that experience, I view reading as far more than just decoding and comprehension. Chambers has provided a tool for constructing whole worlds of insight.

Tell Me: One Application

Listen as a kindergarten class of a few years ago encounters *In the Night Kitchen* by Maurice Sendak. I like this book and had read it to other classes, but on this day and with this particular class, the book hit a nerve. I could tell from the electricity in the room that the children needed to talk. I wasn't prepared at all for where the conversation went.

I began by asking the children what they liked about the book. Their responses ranged from the pictures where Mickey was naked to the chant "Milk in the batter, Milk in the Batter" to Mickey flying the airplane to the end, where Mickey is back in bed safe and sound. They did not like it when Mickey was inside a milk container, when he was falling out of his clothes, and when he was being baked in the cake. The general sense was that these things were scary, especially the part where he is inside the milk container.

The children were puzzled by the things they didn't like: "How could he breathe?" they asked. At first, I thought that was the big puzzle, but they weren't finished. There were deeper fears, deeper puzzles. After a few variations on wondering how he could breathe, Brenda finally spit out the issue that bothered the class the most: How could his parents leave him in the milk? Where were they? Were the bakers really his parents? Who were the bakers?

They also commented on simple patterns, such as the repeated "Milk in the batter." With some prompting on my part (Did you see anything happening over and over?), they also pointed out that Mickey "keeps falling"; he falls out of bed, he falls into milk. Alex noticed that Mickey had "one adventure after another."

Bit by bit, however, the class returned to deeper questions, one question following another. They worried about being abandoned, then about being hurt by bad people when their parents weren't around, and finally, about why there were bad people at all. "How come the police couldn't catch them?" asked Micheal. "Why weren't there police in the book?" I could only sit and acknowledge the questions. They weren't really asking me and seemed to know that what they were asking verged on the unanswerable.

I wondered where this discussion was going and how I was going to get out of it gracefully. For a second or two, I considered just trying, however awkwardly, to end it. Just then, the discussion shifted as one child speculated that the book is all about a bad dream. A debate ensued and, whether out of relief or conviction, they decided that it is about a bad dream. I was just about to open my mouth to sum up, when they went off on another tangent: Where do bad dreams come from? How about bad thoughts, when you think about doing something bad but don't do it? Finally the questions and the discussion wound down.

Not all discussions are so intense and yet, after this one, the class seemed changed. They were more confident, as if they had come through a great adventure. They did more storytelling, wrote more, and asked more questions than they had before. It was a transforming moment for all of us.

The children were able to articulate their fears and worries, and speak about the puzzling and mysterious nature of the world. They took control of what they did not know and made it external to themselves by making it visible. They had an audience, which made the discussion both safer and more powerful. The fact that it was a communal effort increased its power. When someone made a point another child had worried about, it reinforced the sense of belonging to a community of inquirers.

Chambers's "Tell Me" approach seems to elicit such moments of magic. Children begin to feel confident in their questions, look to each other for answers, and challenge the teacher and even the author in their quest. After an experience like this, children are transformed. Their view of themselves and their world can never be the same.

Listening In on Play

Gareth Matthews and Matthew Lipman both discuss the need to listen closely for moments when philosophic inquiry may be taking place. Play is one forum that continues to strive for respectability, particularly in an era of standardized tests. Yet, remarkable questions come up during play. If not always fully articulated, they are unmistakably present. All they need is an audience.

I can vividly remember Donnie, a six-year-old boy whose parents were locked in an unfriendly relationship. Over a period of weeks I watched as he played out scripts around a small house center. The mini-dramas he created jumped around, but most had a mother, a father, children, and pets. There were arguments and sometimes the police showed up, as I assumed they did in real life. Sometimes the mother was the villain of the piece and sometimes it was the father. Other children would occasionally join in the play but Donnie was still running the script. The children who watched did comment on the unfolding drama, sometimes taking sides, sometimes adding their own experience.

The play stopped for a while, but I had the sense that it was not finished. Sure enough, one day I saw Donnie back at the house center. Listening in, I noted the familiar characters and one new one: God was looking down. As the drama unfolded, it turned out that God was mad at both parents. The action jumped, and then God was not mad because the parents had stopped fighting and were being nice to each other. The script shifted again and God was yelling at the parents saying, "How can you be good *and* bad?"

It was a stunning piece of play. I sensed that my role was to listen but not comment. In effect, Donnie was meditating on how people could be good and bad at the same time, on the relationship of God to the world and the world to God. Children are capable of asking fundamental questions—about the nature of reality, how we know things, how we should live our lives, and so on. These are the questions of philosophy.

Children are also capable of searching for deep answers. Melody had become particularly intrigued by Donnie's play. At home she asked her parents why there were bad people in the world and whether bad people were made "bad" by bad thoughts or by bad actions. This had been triggered inadvertently by my insistence that children in the class doing something inappropriate should think harder and use their "brains to make better choices." From this she inferred that there must be "bad brains," something I never said (now I am a lot more careful to define what I mean, one of the important considerations in any philosophical discussion).

However, that is not where this story is leading. Melody went home and solicited her parents' opinions. She reported back to the whole class on their opinions as well as her own. This set off another small round of discussion and a *lot* interesting play over the following days. Even children not involved in the original discussions became involved. This time it was Donnie who was doing the watching and commenting.

Good guys and bad guys were everywhere, but this time they also had good brains and bad brains. Then someone, I don't know who, had the wonderful idea of having bad ideas on purpose. Children tripped over things they should have seen (like other children), walked into walls, and generally made mistakes. Eventually it all died down, but it proved to be another transforming moment in the class. There was a greater degree of cohesiveness in the class, and while Donnie's life was not necessarily easier, he was more a part of the class. And why not? He had asked one of his own deepest questions and even received an answer—of sorts.

A Death in the Classroom

Questions also arise during unhappy moments. The first step in encouraging children to ask questions is to create an environment where support is given and taking risks is rewarded, where we ask the questions with children instead of at them. This means coming up next to the child drawing away from a painting and wondering aloud about what she'll do next. It involves going up to the learner throwing the ball, empathizing with his frustration, and pondering ways to throw the ball farther. It may even involve modeling the body language of questions—the shrug, the hands in the air, the furrowed brow.

But it may also involve standing or sitting beside the child, waiting until they show a sign, verbally or nonverbally, of a question. At this moment a teacher tries to give support. The question, not the answer, is the goal. Teachers who do this are ''lending their consciousness'' to the moment of questioning and providing emotional calm during an instance of unsettlement. It is identical to the interaction of the caregiver and the infant. And it is not just a one-to-one encounter. I've often seen teachers create a setting in which the group's questions are recorded but not necessarily answered. In this way they validate the very act of asking questions.

One year we had twenty duck eggs in an incubator in the classroom. We counted down on a calendar to the expected day of hatching. I needed the preparation as much as the children: twenty-some ducklings in a kindergarten can cause happy but incessant chaos. We read books about duck eggs. We asked questions about ducks: What do they eat? Where do they live? and Where will they go after they hatch?

As we candled the eggs, we discarded several that would not become ducks because they had clearly not developed. The children asked, ''What happened to those eggs?'' ''Are you sure they won't hatch?'' and ''How many do we have left?'' I could sense the unarticulated fears behind these questions.

What we were not prepared for was the complete failure of any of the eggs to hatch. Breaking this kind of news to kindergarten children is not a happy prospect. I struggled over how to do it. I had shared some of the questions the class had asked about ducklings, but this set of questions was mine. What analogy could I use, what story, what information? How could I make it make sense? I did my best, but I could see they were confused. When I told them I was puzzled too, they began to fire questions and speculate about who might have done what to the eggs.

What could have happened? (Not enough heat/light? Too much heat and light? Did they get enough food in the egg? How did they get food in the egg? Did I, as the teacher, know how they got food? If I didn't understand, maybe that was why the eggs didn't hatch.) The very act of telling them I was bewildered opened up the discussion and allowed a therapeutic moment. They returned to questions more than once over the next few days. In the end, Nicolas, a four-year-old, raised his hand. "I know what happened. I remember at my house we were eating eggs. Once we had an egg with blood in it. We couldn't eat that egg because it was no good." Bit by bit, other egg stories came out, eggs that had been left out of the refrigerator, eggs that froze, eggs that went bad, a whole carton that were rotten. They constructed an explanation. It may not have been the right one, and indeed a chart of unanswered questions drifted around the classroom for a long while. (Maybe someday, one of the students may remember these questions and connect them with new knowledge.)

There was still one last piece, the deeper, more fundamental questions that hid behind the anxious, "what happened" questions. These were the "why" questions. Why do things die? Why do people die? Why do pets die? Where do eggs go that do not hatch? Why do people get so sad? Why did the eggs have to leave their mommies and daddies? Deep fears surfaced. Little discussions ensued. Stories about the death of pets went on for days and then debates about whether pets went to heaven or just people.

Egg questions returned and comments that had the flavor of moral ground rules. "People should know everything about an egg before they have them," said Bonita. Alex disagreed, pointing out that we didn't know everything about the gerbils in the class and they were still alive. Besides, he said, "How can you know everything? It's too big!" I couldn't believe my ears. Philosophy was breaking out all over. In the curious rhythms that mark a class, however, the discussion soon began to wane, but it was a wild ride while it lasted.

The class worked together to construct knowledge over time, developing a sense of mutual inquiry. Asking questions gave them power and control in dealing with disturbing ideas. Many questions were left for other days, and I wondered if, for some, they would turn into a quest.

Caroline Earns the Penny

Questions can also act as catalysts for wide-ranging discussion. The media in all its forms are a good source of such questions, and I have wondered why this is so. My best guess is that they are like a distorted mirror of ourselves. On close inspection, we can see things we wouldn't have seen otherwise.

I like to ask questions that engage and puzzle. I'll ask young children, "Is a computer alive?" I'll ask older children, "Are you like a computer? Or not like a computer?" Lately, I've also asked a few children if they could tell whether the person who sent them e-mail was a boy or a girl, an adult or a child. This kind of inquiry is based on the work of Sherry Turkle (1984, 1995), a researcher who has long concerned herself with these issues.

Wrestling with tricky questions leads children to consider identity, thinking, and reality. I try to let discussion proceed, even if in fits and starts, without coming to immediate conclusions to give children a chance to do some necessary and worthwhile thinking. Still, I wasn't prepared for what happened the day I asked a question (passed on to me by a colleague, Dede Sinclair) that has become a personal favorite: "Is Mickey Mouse a mouse, a real person, or just a cartoon? Or is it all of these? Or none of these?" I witnessed one of the greatest single demonstrations of thinking I have ever seen in any grade.

There was a couple of rounds of preliminary discussion. The question puzzled, even troubled, the kindergarten, and called clearly held assumptions into question. One group held that Mickey Mouse was human because one child had seen a cartoon character take off its head at an amusement park; many children found this evidence persuasive. Another view considered Mickey a cartoon figure. Their evidence was the pictures on the clothes and toys they owned. A third, less popular, view was that Mickey was a mouse after all. I am sure that not everyone understood the question, but because it offered options, they could all find an opinion to vote on.

There were some attempts to relate Mickey to other cartoon characters and their reality or cartoon-ness. I wondered aloud if characters in books were real. The general opinion was that they were not real but that they "sounded real a lot of the times but not all of the times." Alex pointed out that "Dr. Seuss books aren't real but they are still books."

I asked this question on and off for about a week, even entertaining the notion of sending it home as a discussion question. Finally, Caroline (of

Chapter 1) got up, marched to the front of the class, informed me that she was going to be the teacher (I guess I wasn't earning the penny again), and began a lecture. Naturally, I didn't have a piece of paper to write down what she said, and of course the whole thing should have been videotaped. What follows is my best summary of a remarkable moment.

Caroline began by holding up two pieces of paper (from the schedule) and saying, "This is Mickey Mouse. It is not a real Mickey Mouse, it is just an imagination one. Someone made it up from their imagination. Maybe Dr. Seuss did it, I don't know! Now suppose this Mickey Mouse is walking down the street and it bites you. But it's not really you, it's an imagination you. You begin to bleed, but only a cartoon you, not the real you. But if there was a real Mickey Mouse in Mickey Mouse clothes, like on Halloween, and it came and bit you, then the real you would be bleeding. It's real and it's not real. And so are you. Understand?"

All while she was saying this, Caroline was holding up the two pieces of paper and gesturing to accompany her words. She went on for a few more minutes with more examples. Sometimes she contradicted herself. I have captured the essence of what she said but neither the eloquence nor the messiness of how she said it. The class listened, enraptured. I may never see anything like it again.

At the end of it, Paulo turned to someone and said, "How did she know that?"

RECOMMENDED READING

Picture Books

Gerstein, Mordecai. *The Mountains of Tibet*. New York: Harper and Row, 1987.

   This is a version of a very well-known folktale. A boy likes to fly kites on the mountain. He grows up, dies, and is offered many choices about who and where he'll be reincarnated. He ends up choosing a very similar life with one exception—in the next life, he chooses to be a girl. My kindergarten class was completely fascinated by the idea of life choices.

Reid, B., and R. Bringhurst. *The Raven Steals the Light*. Vancouver, Toronto, Seattle: Douglas and McIntyre, University of Washington Press, 1984.

   Should Raven steal the light to help the people? There are many versions of this story and many trickster stories, but this one has Raven stealing the sun so that the whole world can enjoy light. Sooner or later comes the question about whether it is right to do a wrong thing for a noble purpose.

Viorst, Judith. *The Tenth Good Thing About Barney.* Illus. Erik Blegvad. New York: Collier Macmillan, 1971.

A basic meditation about coming to terms with the death of a pet. For children it hits very close to home. It always generates discussion about the possibility of an afterlife. More interesting to me is how much young children agree about the possibility of an afterlife.

Reference Books

Chambers, Aidan. *Tell Me: Children, Reading, and Talk.* York, ME: Stenhouse Publishers, 1996; Markham, ON: Pembroke Publishers, 1996.

A slim, easy to read book that lays out a reading program to develop meaningful response in children. The approach is simple, the results profound. I consider this book essential to a thinking classroom.

Matthews, Gareth B. *Dialogues with Children.* Cambridge, MA: Harvard University Press, 1984.

———. *The Philosophy of Childhood.* Cambridge, MA: Harvard University Press, 1994.

Although I really enjoy some of Lipman's work on children and philosophy, I would recommend these books as introductory readings. Each is divided into topics or themes that are fleshed out with anecdotes, observations, and techniques. The tone is friendly, even for those with no background in philosophy.

Paley, Vivian Gussin. *You Can't Say You Can't Play.* Cambridge, MA: Harvard University Press, 1992.

In Paley's books, children grapple with deeper issues through play, but this one had a particular effect on me and on my classroom. It has formed the basis (as it does in Paley's classroom) for a discussion about whether or not it is fair to exclude others in certain circumstances.

Turkle, Sherry. *The Second Self: Computers and the Human Spirit.* New York: Simon and Schuster, 1984.

Written years ago by computer-age standards, this book remains a source of amazing insights into the relation between humans and the computer. It is also the source of some of the questions I ask children to get them to deeper issues about the media.

8

Interlude: Wanting to Know About Knowing

I often do not tell children the truth, and I consider it a sign of progress when they do not tell it to me. Allow me to explain.

Marena was bright—very bright—and immensely logical. She had passions that not every kindergarten child would have, ranging from the *Titanic* to van Gogh. Still, I caused her occasional distress because I so clearly did not tell the truth.

From time to time, I played small practical jokes, tugging on people's hair and pretending to eat it. The children would of course catch me doing this and when they did, I would not only deny it but would point to someone else and say they did it. Children are familiar with this kind of behavior among themselves but it was surprising in an adult.

One day, a student asked me why I was doing what I was doing. I replied that I liked to eat hair because I was an alien. Now to be sure, I don't start off the year with this information, and not every child in kindergarten really understands what it means. Jonathon, for example, was oblivious to all discussions about the subject, since they didn't affect the schedule, and that was the only part of the day he cared about at the time. However, the more mature five-year-olds were immensely engaged by this fiction—particularly by trying to disprove it. It became a kind of logic contest. Students would push me for information and even more outlandish claims in order to catch me in some total implausibility or in some contradiction of what I'd said before. This isn't such an easy game to play, since the collective memory of kindergarten children is pretty impressive.

They wondered how I could look human if I was really an alien. I said I took human pills. They wondered what would happen if I stopped taking the human pills. Would they be able to see me in alien form? I said my principal would get mad at me for being an alien. They said they'd write me a note saying it was okay. On and on it went.

The game was playful, but it prompted some meditations on reality and the nature of truth. Marena, in particular, was interested in proving me wrong. I began encouraging her to prove I was not an alien. Eventually, clever child that she was, she came back with a counter point: since I claimed alien status, it was up to me to prove it. "Prove it" became the general chant in that particular kindergarten.

Eventually, of course, some of the children turned the tables on me. I looked up one day to see Faiza and Amy wandering around with little circles taped on their eyelids and homemade tails taped to their backs.

"What's going on," I asked, not entirely sure I wanted to know.

"We're aliens," announced Amy. "We've come to take over the school!"

"You're not aliens," I said.

"Oh yeah?" Faiza said. "How do you know?"

L. S. Vygotsky (1962) argued over fifty years ago that schools were instrumental in making children aware of their own thinking. Certainly over the last decade or so, there has been a lot of research into how children develop metacognitive awareness and skill in using this awareness to further their learning (see, for example, Flavell et al. 1995). Some programs have endeavored to teach such awareness (see Pressley 1992).

But what interests me most is how such understanding develops naturally. In that regard, the researcher who has caught my attention is Janet Wilde Astington, who claims that "Surprises, secrets, tricks, and lies all depend on understanding and manipulating what others think and know" (1993, p. 98). Obviously, the discussions about aliens fit in here. The question "How do you know?" is only asked by someone who is aware not

Figure 8a   Faiza as an alien. She never told me where she got the idea that aliens looked like this.

only of her own thinking but also of mine. It implies that this learner has a sense of understanding, and tricks, surprises, and humor rely on a sophisticated understanding of the difference between what is said or done and what is meant.

In other words, tricks, humor, and questions have an inherent cognitive value.

And of course, they're also fun.

DISRUPTING EXPECTATIONS AND GENERATING QUESTIONS

Simply breaking a routine—moving materials from their expected place, calling a name that does not exist at attendance, handing out any unfamiliar assignment—can cause the kind of surprise that leads to questions.

One critical decision teachers have to make is when to shake up expectations. I have never discovered a good rule to guide me in doing this, but I have taken advantage of the structures I've put in place—the routines, patterns, and scripts.

One day, for example, I was asked to demonstrate an activity that would lead a class of young children to ask questions. I brought in a large amount of baking soda, a large amount of vinegar, lots of water, and lots of cups. As the children sat in a circle and watched expectantly, I said nothing.

I began by pouring some vinegar in a cup and smelling it myself. I then turned to the child on my left and gestured to her to do the same. She sniffed and made a face. The second child was less sure she wanted to try.

"What's it smell like?" she asked her friend.

"My grandmother's bathroom," the girl replied after a few seconds of consideration.

Apparently intrigued, the second child sniffed. "Cat pee!" she screamed. "Your grandmother uses cat pee?" she asked the first girl. "No," replied the first girl, who then asked me, "It's not cat pee is it?" I shook my head no, thus preventing a riot.

By this time there was a steady clamor. Everyone wanted to smell the mysterious substance. A few questions—what was it and why didn't I talk—floated around. Couldn't I talk? Someone had a grandmother who didn't talk. Grandmothers and my not talking held their attention until I took the next step and poured vinegar into a cup with some baking soda. It immediately fizzed over the side of the cup, to the oohs and ahhs of a class.

I repeated the process by giving each a child a cup and some baking soda, which I motioned them to feel, and some vinegar. By now, the excitement was almost tangible in the room. Questions of all kinds poured out: What happened? What made that? How come its fizzing? Why did that happen? They began to build on one another. I acknowledged as many as possible with a nod. Then, to make things even more interesting, I repeated the whole process, but this time I used water instead of vinegar. There was no fizzing, and there were more questions about that.

I had arranged to leave some vinegar and baking soda behind. The children, prompted by their teacher, said their good-byes. On the way out the door, I turned and said, "Good-bye." As I walked out, I could hear more questions as the children realized that I could talk—but didn't.

Questions and Knowing

It is not necessary to go to this extreme, but by not talking I left a space for the children's questions. I also invited questions through my body language by waiting expectantly and patiently for them to come. In developing inquiry, this was a worthwhile activity, yet in many respects it was also about learning to know. The children considered me a source of knowledge even though I did not speak. *They* knew that *I* knew some answers.

I know I've said this before but questions do not necessarily need an answer, but they do need an audience. Listening to a question, acknowledging a question, or eliciting one from a learner, validates it. Listening affirms the identity of the learner *as* a learner, as one who inquires. It also affirms and nurtures the learner's curiosity. Without this base, children cannot move forward to examine their own cognition or consider the cognition of others. Once questions are understood as tools, children can treat them as they treat the work in a portfolio—as evidence that they have a brain.

Tricks

Ashley and Sandra were inseparable. They drew, painted, and put on puppet shows together. They also began to play practical jokes. The most memorable one nearly gave me a heart attack. They took cotton, meticulously dyed the end of it red, placed the cotton in their noses, and for good measure dabbed the end of their noses red. Then they began to practice crashing into each other in the most comic ways. I saw them practicing the crashes, but I didn't see the cotton. After one particularly good pratfall, they brought out the cotton. For an instant I was taken in. That was enough for them. They screamed with laughter, and so did everyone watching me. It was a magnificent piece of comic timing.

I asked children who saw the incident if Ashley and Sandra were lying to me or tricking me, and how you could tell the difference. It wasn't an easy question and there was some on and off discussion about it during the following week. Each time they played a trick, there was a little more to talk about. Finally, Sandra said that the difference was if the person playing the joke meant it as a joke. This struck most of the class as a good answer.

A day later, however, when someone played a joke the other child didn't find at all humorous, the discussion revived, but with a sharper focus. This time they understood that it had to be a joke, but they also saw that the person receiving it had to find it funny. The children wondered if this was the difference between lying and tricking: a lie is something that is not funny but a trick is.

Now this, to be sure, is only one aspect of the difference between tricking and lying, but it brings up another point. I sometimes come across the claim that children can't be considered artists because they do what they do to please themselves instead of considering an audience (see Gardner 1980). In this case, however, the girls knew they were tricking me and had planned the effect for an audience. When children develop an understanding of what a trick is, they are making a basic distinction between reality and fantasy, between something and thinking about something. This kind of thought process is a useful strategy for learners who havent yet developed many reflective skills.

It was in this milieu of trick-playing that Jonathon made another discovery as significant as finding the future. He came to me one day complaining of a stomachache. He rolled his eyes, clutched his stomach, and moaned. He hadn't appeared unwell earlier, but I reached for his forehead. As I did, Jonathon broke into a wide grin and said, "Ha! Tricked you!" He was enormously pleased with himself, and with good reason. After all, it was his brain that had done the tricking, and at some deep level he *knew* it.

HUMOR AND SYMBOL SYSTEMS

Through trickery children learn about the social conventions of appropriate behavior, but they also learn about knowing. More important to me, however, is the humor and laughter it sets off in the classroom. When appropriate humor is allowed into the classroom, many children come alive. I remember Amy as very quiet and reserved. She was always standing in the shadow of her friend Caroline, and I wondered if she would disappear when Caroline moved away. She didn't, of course, and what's more, she began to assume some of Caroline's functions in leading the singing and dancing that broke out at any time that year. She also began to display a sense of humor all her own.

One day, late in the winter of the year, she stared at my wedding band and said, "Are you married?" I shrugged and confirmed that I was. She slapped her head, reeled backwards and said, "Oh my God!"

Figure 8b   The marriage announcement. Amy was positive that such an announcement had to be "neat," so she put in the lines.

I didn't know if this meant "Oh no, the bottom of the barrel and it's gone already" or "Oh no, my teacher has a life," or what. I wasn't even sure if it was real news to her or not. However, it *was* something she was going to make as much of as she could. She told practically every member of the class, who reacted with everything from horror to incomprehension. She spun around for a little while and then announced, with a gleam in her eye, that she was going to make an announcement about it. With some assistance, she wrote out the announcement and carried it to the principal, who was very good and showed Amy that she was putting it with the next day's announcements.

The next morning Amy sat with her hands folded on the table (the only time I'd ever seen her like that), suppressing a huge grin. The vice-principal, who had no context for the announcement, read it as straight news. Amy got up without saying a word.

Pandemonium broke out. Emergency meetings of the school social committee were called to discuss what was appropriate in cases where a wedding had already taken place. Students came up to me all day and congratulated me, and so did parents. It was all the more awkward because I have been married for years.

I reported all this chaos to Amy a few days later. She said nothing for a moment. Then, eyebrows raised, with a straight face, she asked, ''Do you have any children?''

Children who use humor are taking themselves from structure to construction. To be funny, one has to have some understanding of conventions and how to bend them. Humor implies that you know some of the formats, the expected routines, and the patterns of an intelligence and its applications. In order to be able to write a parody of a folktale, a learner has to know the conventions. In order to make up new words to a familiar melody, one has to understand the rhythm of that melody. In Amy's case, she knew (or came to know) the social conventions of making an announcement, and she certainly was aware that she was being funny.

Using humor involves a lot of creative thinking. It takes material out of context, substitutes new words, images, or gestures, and exaggerates meanings. It engages the imagination of both the humorist and the audience. It fills the classroom with the sound of children's laughter.

RECOMMENDED READING

Astington, Janet. *The Child's Discovery of Mind.* Cambridge, MA: Harvard University Press, 1993.

A very readable account of the ways in which children come to know about their own thinking. The author grounds her observations in many anecdotes and observations of children in conversation and covers a wide array of topics related to knowing. I have returned to it several times in order to understand some of my own conversations with children.

Margulies, Nancy. *Mapping Inner Space: Learning and Teaching Mind Mapping.* Tucson, AZ: Zephyr Press, 1991.

One of the more effective ways of teaching children about their own thinking is through the use of visual organizers. This book combines the use of visual organizers with talk about thinking. I have found it very useful with children above kindergarten age.

Seuss, Dr. *Oh the Thinks You Can Think.* New York: Random House Beginner Books, 1975.

A lesser-known work, this book directly addresses thinking and the imagination. I generally read it with young children early in the year to introduce the idea of ''brain talk'' and return to it every few months as the children's appreciation of their own thinking grows.

9

Touching Intelligence: Experience

But, above all, touch teaches us that life has depth and contour; it makes sense of the world and ourself as three-dimensional. Without that intricate feel for life there would be no artists, whose cunning is to make sensory and emotional maps, and no surgeons, who dive through the body with their fingers.

DIANE ACKERMAN

A Natural History of the Senses

Mary arrived in my grade six class one year from a rural part of Guyana. She was sociable and outgoing and made friends easily. She had a real aptitude for drawing and could concentrate on a drawing project for long periods of time. Her academic skills, however, were very limited and she surely had many frustrating days in addition to adjusting to a new culture.

Studying an ancient civilization is part of the grade six program, and we were concentrating on the Aztecs, the Incas, and the Mayas. As part of this course of study, we arranged a trip to the Royal Ontario Museum. There, children were actually able to touch and examine artifacts of the period. The class was impressed by the age of the objects and the skill and cleverness of their construction. At some level, they began to have an emotional appreciation of these cultures by handling their tools.

One especially interesting artifact was a stone bowl and pestle. No one could really guess at its purpose except Mary. She knew immediately that it was for grinding herbs and corn, making a type of bread, and two or three other uses, which she explained in great detail. She knew because she had done these things all the time as a little girl. I was furiously taking notes, and the lady from the museum was also paying close attention to the little demonstration. The rest of the class, who'd always liked Mary, looked ready to cheer. The thinking she described was intricate and full of cautions (You have to be careful not to do this . . .) and explanations (It works because the bowl is still hot).

This incident served as an important lesson about "experiential" learning. If we want children to demonstrate what they know, we really do need to surround them with objects and artifacts. These are the tools of thinking, the physical manifestations of symbol systems.

*M*any teachers make it a point to include experiential learning in their classroom. They set up nature corners, science centers, or areas with construction materials as part of the class environment or as part of a study unit. At my school, we also go on trips to museums to extend children's learning. In doing so, we are providing opportunities for what Howard Gardner calls the experiential entry point—learning by doing.

The idea that authentic experience is vital to the educational enterprise is not new. Early in this century, John Dewey (1966) argued strongly for the value of such work. Yet this kind of learning is often considered a mere add-on rather than a core element of education. In part, this may stem from the fact that such experiences are not embedded or mandated in the everyday curriculum. At a deeper level, however, is the perception that working with the hands is just not cognitively challenging enough.

MUSEUMS

An excellent framework for understanding and implementing experiential learning is the idea of the "classroom as museum." Gardner's advocacy of museums as a powerful form of learning strikes a deep chord in me because I remember the feeling of learning while being in a museum as a child. Even as an adult I find "hands-on" museums a lot of fun and enjoy interacting with the exhibits as much as the students. A tangible community of inquiry springs up among adults and children on field trips to such places.

One of my favorite early memories is going to the Children's Museum in Boston the late 1960s. Among many vivid exhibits, there was a full-scale model of a sewer you could actually go into. For the first time, I realized that cities rest on an underground base that carries water and electricity. I wondered who had thought of such things. It inspired me to think of putting electricity underground to heat sidewalks and melt snow.

This kind of recollection can drive personal reflection many years later. It poses ongoing questions about how things work. I never really pursued my thoughts about sewers and cities, but I was aware of them. A few years ago, when I noticed a student poring over David Macauley's (1976) *Underground,* I was reminded of some of these questions. I spent some time considering the book with a small group of children, each of us adding our own background knowledge. We never formalized this discussion in any way, but it was fascinating to see how alive the learning from all those years ago still was.

It would be great if we could all rush over to the corner "interactive museum" to pursue questions like this when the need arises, but we are lucky to visit such places even once a year. Yet, if the evidence of my own life is any indication, this kind of experience is very durable. Gardner's point that schools and classrooms need to look more like museums is a logical—and powerful—one.

Bit by bit, we have tried to incorporate the museum idea in our classroom. As we have discovered, it helps to think about how interactive museums work. Consider what happens at such a museum. An exhibit may be about baseball. Visitors can touch or throw an object like a baseball. A computer supplies information about how fast the ball is moving. There may be additional displays about how baseballs are made, how they curve when thrown, and how fast they can go when thrown. An interactive museum provides some of the tools of intelligence, direction in at least one investigation, and feedback and further extensions.

Any interactive classroom museum therefore invites exploration and investigation of tools, objects, and collections. These can range from computer parts to paintings to leaves. As teachers, we supply the interactive part—the challenges, the questions, and the feedback to learning. You'd think this was obvious, but as the saying goes, we learn from experience.

Discovery Boxes

Following on the idea that schools need to be more museumlike, Carol, my teaching partner, and I became really interested in the Royal Ontario Museum's discovery boxes. These are wooden boxes, each on a separate topic (such as birds, feathers, or magnets) and each containing materials relevant to that topic, such as instructions, suggestions, information, actual materials to study and use, and tools such as a magnifying glass. The boxes are stored on shelves, and children can select one and take it to a nearby table.

We were intrigued by the idea and set out to make our own discovery boxes for the kindergarten classroom. As with all things, however, we made a few false starts. Magnets are fun, but if the pieces are too small they get lost. If more than one box is out on the table, materials get mixed up. Eventually, however, a couple of discovery areas took hold.

The most popular was the vision box, which contained materials that played with or distorted visual effects: little prisms, telescopes, and eye pieces. One eye piece let you look straight ahead but you're really seeing at a 90-degree angle. There was a do-it-yourself kaleidoscope and spinning disks that made kaleidoscopic patterns on their own.

It was an instant success. Alex was fascinated by the 90-degree eye piece and wandered around the classroom suddenly turning at right angles. Amy, visual child that she was, spun the several kaleidoscopic disks at once and pronounced herself ''dizzy'' (I couldn't even watch her do it). Other children discovered pirates when they peered through the telescope. One of our challenges to the children was to make a picture of something they had seen. This produced some remarkable attempts at representing kaleidoscopic effects.

Another challenge asked children to use the instruments in strange ways. I'd ask, ''What will happen if you turn something around or use it the wrong way?'' Sometimes the effect was uninteresting but when we turned the telescope around, it created a lot of excitement. ''How could you get bigger one way and smaller the other?'' Caroline demanded. Alex was perplexed that he could see through the 90-degree eye piece one way but not the other way. The most exciting discovery, of course, was the children's. It involved putting one of the kaleidoscopic spinning disks into the make-your-own kaleidoscope device. The result was a kaleidoscope that spun and changed patterns at a very high speed. As if this weren't enough, some children remembered that if you twirled yourself around you get the same

Figure 9a   Amy made a copy of what her hand looked like through a kaleidoscopic lens.

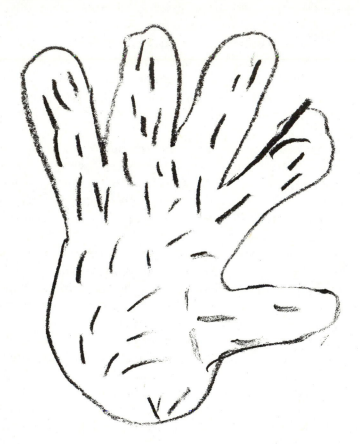

sensation of dizziness. They put on colored material and became kaleido-scopes themselves. They couldn't spin forever, of course. Eventually, they moved on to other pursuits. But my head was left spinning by the possibili-ties contained in this little box.

Entering Science Through Discovery Boxes

Carol and I began to show our discovery boxes to other teachers. Among them were Lynn Alloi, a grade one teacher who had come to our "teacher as researcher" program, and Peter Gillis, a grade three/four teacher. When they saw our work-in-progress, they made their own discovery boxes. In the process, they raised them to another level.

In Lynn's class, there was immediate (and sometimes overwhelming) enthusiasm for the discovery boxes. Her grade ones spent hours engrossed in experimentation and discussion. Lynn also found that her students were more likely to write and draw their observations with discovery boxes than with any other material.

Peter decided to use the boxes to teach various ways of discovering through different intelligences. He began by asking the children to look into the clear plastic boxes and predict what was common about all the items they saw. Then he asked them to make a simple inventory of the items, a clever idea for keeping track of the contents as well as a good way to begin exploring the materials.

The boxes contained a range of small, inexpensive materials. In the time box, for example, there were a few stopwatches and a few starter activities like timing how long it took to say the alphabet. In the power box, they found wires, light bulbs, and leftover Polaroid cartridge packs (which still have a battery charge).

Peter had no firm expectations about what children might do or not do with the contents of the boxes, but they amazed him with marvelous investigations. One group attempted to count the floor tiles in the hallway within a certain length of time. A very social student organized a group around the power box. It wasn't clear at first what was happening, but it turned out that the students, including beginning English speakers, had arranged a demonstration. They began to sing "This Little Light of Mine" while the beginning English speakers turned the lights on and off in time to the music. A teacher can't possibly think of this kind of discovery. Children have to invent it.

Peter was also interested in how to get children to report their discoveries in ways that would acknowledge and honor the different intelligences. As groups rotated from box to box, he demonstrated ways of responding visually, physically, musically, and so on. The class went on to discuss different ways of being smart.

The results were startling. Children made pictures showing who did what and where, indicating a keen social and visual awareness. Some physically acted out the results of their experiments—for example, acting like gyroscopes, spinning on one foot with arms extended. And this kind of work transferred over to other areas. Children began to discuss characters in books according to their intelligences, and to reflect on their own and, in so doing, probably became more sensitive to others.

The boxes were meant to facilitate an understanding of science, but they also led children to discover themselves.

BUILDING IN CHALLENGES

One of the communities in my classroom is a group of builders. Energetic and usually cooperative, they never seem to run out of ideas for big block building projects. When they do they consult photographs of the efforts of past classes. In one of these photographs, a small ramp leading up to a structure gave Blaine an idea. He wanted to test how far a car would go on different ramps. He and the group got to work. I would occasionally come by and ask questions: "Can you angle the ramp up too high?" or "Does it make any difference which car you use?" The children would ponder these things and report back their findings.

In the end, these young builders concluded that the steeper the decline, the faster and farther the car went (best of all, the faster it went, the better the crash). Metal cars did go farther (and crash better), but if the angle was too high, the car would just go straight down. This was an eloquent example of learning. Blaine, in particular, was already expressing a lot of understanding for a four-year-old.

It was only a matter of time before the group thought of a new idea. This time, the cars would go in the other direction. Soon small plastic cars were zooming *up* the ramp. The children realized that long, low ramps could launch a car a fair distance but that it wouldn't go too high.

I was a little leery but the group was being careful. Then I asked them to come up with their own challenge. They conferred and decided to make a ramp that made a car go "straight up." I thought about it and gave my approval, but with the proviso that the car could not hit the ceiling. Now which cars were best at going up? Would it still be the metal ones? We struck a bargain.

All seemed to be well until I heard a shriek coming from the bathroom, which had a cubicle with high doors. Sure enough, a car had landed on someone in the cubicle. In the ensuing discussion of the incident, one child finally informed me that the toilet itself had been the target not the person on the toilet. The group thought having a target would be a good challenge—after all, I said not to hit the *ceiling*. I didn't say anything about the toilet, and besides, it was a plastic car—the group was of the opinion that it might float.

I should have taken more time to consider all the angles.

Figure 9b   Basic write-ups and observations from Peter's class on discovery boxes.

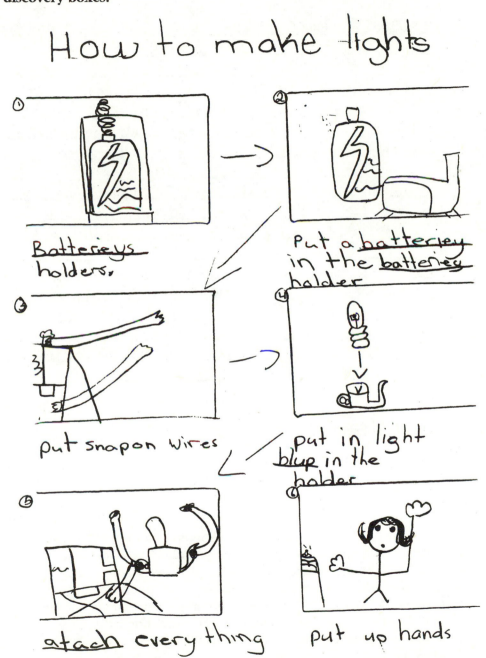

How to make lights

① Battereys holders,

② Put a batteriey in the batteriey holder

③ put snapon wires

④ put in light blup in the holder

⑤ atach every thing

⑥ put up hands

Figure 9b   continued

Respone to Power Box   May 30 19

I liked the new batteries because it works better.
I liked the multi-colored wires because they make
everything works. I like the light bulb because it
has shiny lights.

I disliked the horn because it didn't work. I don't
like the wire cutters because I don't like cutting wires
I don't like the red wire because it doesn't work.

How do they make the horn work? How do they make camera
batteries. How do they make the ligh bulbs?

The horn reminded me of my bikes horn. The wire
reminds me of my wires. The wire cutters reminded me of my
scissors.

Play-Debrief-Replay

Wasserman (1988, 1990) speaks of a "play-debrief-replay" paradigm for
play- and science-based activities. It's a framework that has worked for me
for a number of years. What I particularly like is that it adds the teacher
to the mix of materials and hands-on experience. *Play* refers to the initial
stage of exploration, discovery, and experimentation with new materials.
Debrief, which follows, consists of inviting the class to discuss their observations, ask questions, and deliver new challenges. Finally, and most important, after the discussion, the teacher sends children back to *replay* their
exploration, this time with a new focus and additional knowledge.

The car ramp is a good example of play-debrief-replay at work. A group
of children started a project on their own initiative. I came by, asked questions, and set down some ground rules to focus the activity. By listening

to their observations, I learned where some of the children were—or could be. The children learned by listening to one another and to the feedback and challenges I gave them.

The debriefing stage can include all kinds of challenges: questions or comments that give immediate feedback or a new criterion (get it over the bathroom wall) that directs performances in new ways. To provide new challenges teachers can always change the materials. We need to consider how to use the debriefing well. After all, an interactive exhibit never stays the same all the time, does it?

It is important to remember that questions or challenges do not have to be "answered" to our satisfaction or according to any deadlines we set. If we push for "correct" answers, we have merely imposed our knowledge on children before they have been able to demonstrate a deeper understanding of what this knowledge is about. And if we ask questions we already know the answers to or are unwilling to listen to children's answers, we also impose our knowledge on them. This is the antithesis of what Gardner intends in an educational system. If a child can't figure out a solution, then these are questions and challenges for another day. The teacher may need to provide some additional demonstrating and modeling or introduce a different set of questions, criteria, or materials. Then again, children may simply need more time.

There are all sorts of places one can turn for examples of ways to challenge children's thinking. Wasserman (1988, 1990) does an excellent job of detailing some of these, as do Morgan and Saxton (1994).

A framework I have used and returned to repeatedly is the SCAMPER model, adapted from *The Child's World: Presenting Design and Technology* (Metropolitan Toronto School Board 1989):

*S*ubstitute: What can be substituted?

*C*ombine: What can be put together?

*A*dapt: How can you change or use something to make it work?

*M*odify, miniaturize, magnify: Can you make some or all of it bigger or smaller? Can some part of it be changed?

*P*ut to other use: Can you use this for something else?

*E*liminate: Can you make do without some part of it?

*R*everse: What would happen if the design or the parts were changed?

This model generates questions and actions to challenge a learner. Although it has specific uses for this the experiential entry point, its applications are almost limitless.

With all of this, how can one ever keep track? Brian Mitchell and Tammy Clark, kindergarten teachers with our board, have devised a solution. They have made lists of the kinds of challenges a teacher can give in different areas of the classroom:

Blocks

Purpose:
This center provides learning opportunities as outlined for all drama centers (enhanced role-playing ability, development of oral language and story telling abilities, cooperation, drawing, and writing) and the Construction Sets (spatial reasoning and awareness of geometric properties, creativity in design, large muscle control). During clean-up the children must sort and classify based on size, shape, and type of blocks. In addition:

To develop mapping skills:
• children record/represent imaginary trips through map making

• children become familiar with mapping symbols

• children begin to understand directions (North/South, left/right, etc.)

Some Questions to Ask:
1. Tell me about what you have made?
2. How did you create this structure?
3. Can you make instructions for another person could make the same structure?
4. How would you use _____?
5. What can you add to _____?

Construction Sets

Purpose:
To develop an awareness of space and geometric properties
To develop creativity and design working within three dimensions—constructions will become increasingly complex to include bridges, roofs, and symmetrical designs
To provide opportunities for dramatic/imaginative play
To develop large and small muscle control
To develop self-expression, oral language (communication skills)
To encourage cooperation and sharing with others
Some Questions to Ask:
1. Tell me about what you have made?

2. How did you create this structure?
3. Why did you choose these materials instead of _____?
4. Can you make instructions for another person to make the same structure?
5. Is there anything else you would like to add?

A public challenge reiterates the idea that learning is based on thinking. In the end, the goal of challenges is to encourage children to come up with their own. (You never know where they will take you.)

Challenging Through Words

We shouldn't go around pestering children with pointless questions that simply rehearse what we want children to know (Morgan and Saxton 1994). Questions have a much greater power: they can direct a child to analyze (Which car went farther?), synthesize (How does the whole thing work?), or predict (Where should the ramp go so the car doesn't go over the bathroom stall?). Genuinely challenging questions are an important part of the debriefing process.

Sometimes, a debriefing session ends with a challenge to increase the specificity of a solution, to supply, for example, a higher level of detail. In studying the Aztecs, my grade five/six class noted their strong preference for indigo blue in their clothing, which led to my challenge that they learn to make that exact shade by mixing colors until they got it right. When some students were making a model of an Aztec temple, the number of stairs in the model had to conform with the actual number. This involved finding out the actual number, but because the steps numbered in the hundreds, we settled on one quarter of that amount for the model.

Another challenge involves making some object meet a certain criterion. When five children were building a car from big blocks, they argued over who would actually get to sit in the finished car. It only took me a few visits to figure out that a challenge was emerging. With some strong directing on my part, the children came up with the idea of making a car with enough seats for all of them. This seemed fair to those involved, and they pursued some productive activity. Better still, the children internalized the challenge and began to make cars that could accommodate as many as eight. They learned about different design possibilities, but they also learned about fairness.

Challenging a group to measure a length of carpet using small cubes or paper clips as units of measurement is one way to introduce the concept of number. I have made construction challenges (create a house that has twenty or thirty or forty pieces). I also "up the ante" by throwing out a cheap stopwatch and asking children to complete a project, such as a large puzzle, in a given amount of time.

Challenges Without Words

Something from Nothing
My classroom has an area we call the "box gluing" center, where children construct things with recycled materials. Almost anything—from tissue boxes to toilet paper cylinders to leftover art materials—is useful. A little glue and imagination produces a wide variety of constructions. We take what comes in from all sources as well as what we can find.

There is no accounting, however, for what children may discover. One day in January, the center was almost empty. Jane came up to ask me if the calendar on the table was an old one or a new one and if it was old could she use it. I said it was last year's and she could have it. A while later I looked over to see her folding bits of paper towel into little squares. On each she was putting a number carefully cut from the calendar. When I asked what she was making, she replied a robot that would find more stuff for the box gluing center. (I suspect that the underlying point was that I wasn't doing my job.)

At our writing-drawing-creating table we deliberately mix paper, string, bits of fabric, staplers, tape, and whatever else is on hand (children practice before they use the tape or the stapler). All these materials invite experimentation and tinkering.

We do not have a craft of the day (or week or month). The children's own creativity produces results ranging from spiders to books. One day I watched a child in Carol's morning class create an entire Halloween outfit of a bumblebee out of construction paper and leftover bits of material. How could we even think up a marvelous project like that?

In other areas, less is more. We do not have a fully set up house center, but we do have materials learners can use to make houses (or cars or restaurants). We want to expose children to materials that do not have obvious or preordained purposes. It forces them to do their own thinking and planning. By assembling materials according to their own mental plan, they can literally make their thinking visible!

Putting Materials Out of Context   Like any classroom, ours has general areas for specific activities, but what we've observed is that materials set out close together are often used together. Knowing this, we might arrange the room so that small building material—plastic and wooden blocks, for example—is near a doll house. We were also blind to some of the perils of this arrangement. The snack table is close to the painting easels. Ordinarily this works well because it gives the painters an audience while they work. The peril is that the snack table can also provide new materials for painting. More than once I've come by the painting area and seen children using crackers, apples, and peanut butter. While I'd prefer they *eat* the snack, the principle is important—materials taken out of context promote creative thinking.

Teachers don't have to leave this kind of creativity entirely to chance: we can put superhero toys at the paint center instead of paintbrushes, giving the toys a new creative use. Pieces of cloth can be used instead of paper, different types of clay and soil instead of paints. These substitutions demonstrate lateral thinking both on the part of the teacher who does the planning and the children who do the creating.

Taking Things Away   In contrast, grade six students experimented with the table hockey game by creating different configurations. They took away the goalies and defenseman, leaving only the little pegs on which the figures sat, which changed the game to high-scoring "shoot-outs," as they called it. In another example, several kindergarten children built tall towers from the big plastic blocks. Then, while I held my breath, they tried taking them away without causing the towers to topple over. (Inevitably, they do).

Less is often more. When you take something away, the work changes, an important consideration in getting children to understand the concept of editing or modifying their work to improve it. Many children are under the misapprehension that the only way to improve something is to add to it. We need to demonstrate otherwise through our questions, comments, and feedback.

COLLECTIONS

A Little Investigation into Leaves

Over time, as the "classroom as museum" idea becomes more familiar, everything becomes a potential collection. We have accumulated computer parts, toy cars, seashells, rocks, instruments of all kinds from different parts of the world, and even an extensive book collection, which is sufficiently large that we never have it all out at once. The classroom is also full of living plants of all kinds, a collection in itself. All these collections, when we make them available, are meant to be handled, used, and discussed.

While out walking one day, I found a really big, red maple leaf. I brought it to class to show students and put a few other leaves nearby for comparison. (It seemed like a good idea at the time.) Then someone asked if he or she could bring in a leaf found on the way to school. Soon, leaves were rolling in, and before I knew what had happened, we had piles and piles, more leaves than we needed for a collection. This is the kind of authentic problem museum curators confront all the time. They have more objects and artifacts than they know what to do with and must develop criteria for selecting exemplary objects. (In hindsight, I realize that this is yet another way the collect/select cycle begins.) We finally had to sort and classify the leaves and then selected exemplars for our collection.

Our discussion stayed relatively simple because there are only so many kinds of trees in our neighborhood. However, as we talked about the deluge of leaves, we all realized that less might be more. The children came up with various criteria, such as smallest, most colored, biggest, most unusual shape. With some prodding, they were also able to combine categories: like biggest and most colored, smallest and most colored, and so on. Andrew summed up the most important lesson the children learned: "I never knew leaves were so hard to understand."

Finding Treasure: Tools of Thinking

In our program, we give a lot of consideration to physical props. We have different types of fabric, shoes, and hats in the dress-up center to encourage investigation into character and characterization. There are magnifying glasses and telescopes that can be used for real and imaginary investigations; scales, measuring cups, counting boards, and rulers; pencils, pens, markers, and paintbrushes. The children can actually use and explore all the musical instruments from different countries. These objects are tools of different symbol systems. They not only help us do the work of a symbol system—painting, calculating, composing—they also help us understand the nature of a symbol system: a piano tells us about music, a paintbrush

Figure 9c   Faiza and Richmond searching for gold, dirt, and adventure. The pyrite was actually in the fish tank behind them.

about painting. Without a range of tools, children cannot investigate or try out the different intelligences.

I never know exactly how these tools will end up being used. One day, there was a lot of noise, even for an active classroom, from a group in the corner. Ambling over to investigate, I was informed that I wouldn't be told what was going on, since it was a secret. I decided to watch. The group appeared to be looking for something, and several children held magnifying glasses in their hands. Soon enough, I heard that that something was "gold." Rocks of all kinds were held up for close scrutiny but each was rejected because it was "not the gold rock." The children huddled in a corner of the classroom that housed fish tanks, rocks of all kinds, and magnifying glasses, including a large one. There was much looking around at the floor with magnifying glasses. (I was informed of how dirty my floor was.)

Lying on the floor, Jordana announced that she saw "sparkly stuff," and several excited children quickly flopped onto the floor next to her. "Maybe the gold has been chopped up," I suggested. "How do you know it's dirt? How do you tell the difference between sparkly dirt and gold?" This struck them as a question worth considering, and soon they were back at it, scrutinizing one rock and then another.

"No way that's gold," Faiza observed. She had looked at her own floor while watching television and noticed the same sparkly stuff. "Besides," she said, "look at the sand in the sandbox—it's sparkly but it's not gold." There was a stampede to the sand table. I asked a few more questions inviting comparison between the sand in the box and the sparkly stuff on the floor, but Richmond delivered the verdict, "That's dirt on the floor."

I went away for a minute or two and when I returned, several children were opening their mouths wide while Faiza peered in through the large magnifying glass. There was some discussion about tongues, throats, and uvulas but, alas, no gold. I asked why they were looking down each other's throats. Had they given up the search for gold? "No," they replied in chorus. "We heard that some people had gold fillings in their teeth," said Faiza. They were disappointed not to find any.

Then they turned to the fish tanks and were surprised at how hard it was to see into them with magnifying glasses. "Hey," I said, "how come it looks different when you look in the side of the tank?" They discussed this, too, and inevitably someone noticed that there were rainbows if you looked into the tank in a certain way. We talked about how light bends and is distorted in the water and around the corners of the tank. To my surprise, Richmond yelled, "Maybe it's the gold!" As I was about to correct him, we saw a piece of pyrite, or "fools gold," in the tank.

I never did figure out who put the pyrite in the tank, but it was clear that there was a lot of learning going on. The proximity of the materials to each other was intended to create some "cross context" investigation, but I was surprised at how the children linked the contexts together. The challenges were limitless, and the children were coming up with their own. In a short time, they had covered the structure of the human mouth, the nature of rocks, dirt, and the world beneath our feet, and the nature of light entering a fish tank. They had used the magnifying glasses to examine parts of the room in new ways. The children had played, pondered, and replayed. Not all days are so productive: this experience would ground class discussions on and off for a week.

Making a Video

Media has to be experienced to really understand it. Children should experience making a form of media, instead of passively consuming it. Make a simple two-minute video with children and they'll never watch the media in the same way again. In a grade three/four class for learners with academic and behavioral concerns, the media were a favorite topic. Late in the year, they had an opportunity to make a small video. We began by collecting toys from the various hamburger chain promotions running at the time. These would serve as props. We then taught children to run a video-camera for one second and then stop. This wasn't too hard for Jeremy, George, and Peter, who learned to run the camera as if they were born to it. As a class, we plotted out a very simple story line—one character drives away in another character's car. (You can plan a longer story line, but you'll find that even something as short as this will take time).

To shoot the video, we placed the props in certain spots, ran the video-camera for a second, stopped, moved the props a fraction of an inch, ran the video-camera again, and so on. During the shoot, the class was as organized and cooperative as I'd ever seen them. They arranged the objects, got out of the way, shot the second of film, and moved the objects again. It all took longer than they expected. They weren't finished even after thirty minutes. All Peter, Jeremy, and George wanted to do was see what they had made to that point. I was really happy with what they had done. As they watched, however, they looked stunned and confused. I asked what was wrong.

Peter answered, "Where are we? How come we aren't in the movie?"

It was my turn to be stunned and confused. "Why did you think you would be in the movie?" I asked. "Because we made it," George answered on behalf of the group.

It seemed an excellent moment to consider their questions, so I invited them to go back and figure out where they were when the camera was shooting the scene. Peter actually had to reposition himself in order to understand that they were under the table while the camera was running.

It is experiences like this that introduce children to the power of creation. When they showed their brief video to friends, all were mesmerized that a video had been made at school. Although they planned to keep their technique a secret, they could barely contain themselves when asked how they did it.

Later, at his desk, Jeremy announced to everyone in general, "I made a movie and I made it with my own hands." He knew "in his bones" that he had learned something. There is no erasing or easy forgetting of that feeling.

RECOMMENDED READING

Picture Books

Cole, Babette. *The Trouble with Dad.* London, UK: Collins Publishing Group, 1987.

Dad is a mad inventor who comes up with all sorts of strange gadgets to solve little problems. Not all of these inventions work out. Still, this demonstration of "lateral thinking" is very funny and may spark a lot of creative ideas.

Williams, Karen Lynn. *Galimoto.* Illus. Catherine Stock. New York: Lothrop, Lee and Sheppard Books, 1990.

A story, set in Africa, about making wire sculptures.

Wynne-Jones, Tim, and I. Wallad. *Architect of the Moon.* Toronto: Douglas and McIntyre, 1988.

When the moon falls apart, a little guy flies up and uses blocks of different shapes and sizes to rebuild it. When we read this book, inevitably children reconstruct what they have seen in the illustrations. It also raises the subject of what an architect is and does, and this has led some children into blueprint making.

Reference Books

Bosak, Susan V. *Science Is . . . A Source Book of Fascinating Facts, Projects and Activities.* Toronto: Scholastic Canada/The Communication Project, 1992.

A resource book of science activities: miniature land ecosystems, mini-aquatic ecosystems, a plan for a mold garden, growing plants without soil, and aerodynamics (paper copters, paper airplanes, other weird flying things). There are many such idea books, but this is one I particularly like.

Cassidy, John. *Explorabook: A Kids' Science Museum in a Book.* Palo Alto, CA: Klutz Press, 1991.

———. *Earthsearch: A Kid's Geography Museum in a Book.* Palo Alto, CA: Klutz Press, 1994.

Interactive museums in book form. These outstanding books are put out by the people associated with the Exploratorium in San Francisco. When I first got them, it took me some time to finish with them myself before letting my class have them. Go ahead, treat yourself, and take a trip to the museum.

Wasserman, Selma. *Serious Players in the Primary Classroom.* New York: Teachers College Press, 1990.

Wasserman, Selma, and J. W. George Ivany. *Teaching Elementary Science: Who's Afraid of Spiders.* Toronto: Harper and Row, 1988.

Both excellent, both featuring the play-debrief-replay model.

10

Interlude: Wondering About the Role of the Body

The ultimate purpose of the human body: to serve as the tool by which the personality is shaped. The teacher can nourish the children's minds and provide good opportunities for the exercise of their emotions, but it is the children's bodies which teach them and which lead them to become the persons they are. The good teacher is the one who can help the children to become fully aware of their physical person and of all they can accomplish. The children who know their instrument well will play it well.

ALICE YARDLEY

Senses and Sensitivity

By all accounts, Jackson had spent most of his time in kindergarten crying. Indeed, when he arrived in the class for learners with language exceptionalities, he was very nervous. He complained that his stomach was upset, retreated to corners, and generally demonstrated no confidence in himself.

He also drew odd-shaped boundaries around his pictures. They were almost a signature of sorts. Eventually, one of the consultants attached to the program, an expert in evaluating children's drawings, pointed out that these were not ordinary shapes around each picture but stomach shapes. Where he had learned to draw stomachs was a mystery, but there was no denying it once we had seen it.

As the year rolled along, Jackson's nervousness subsided. There was a lot of emphasis in this class on using boxes, old clothes, and furniture to construct dramatic play. Sensory experiences, such as playing in shaving cream, experimenting with soap solutions, and eating a wide variety of food were an intrinsic part of the program.

As a learner with many strengths, Jackson began to use the program to learn to cope and compensate. As the year came to a close, he wasn't exactly confident but neither was he hiding in corners. There were fewer stomachs outlining his drawings.

Returning in the fall, Jackson had changed in both tangible and intangible ways. Confident, even aggressive at times, he talked, took risks, and was generally on his way to a spectacular year of progress. While we were thrilled by these developments, we were also puzzled. We asked his parents if they noticed a difference or had an explanation.

Yes, they said, they had noticed a difference, but they couldn't really think of any reason for the change. The only thing that had happened was that Jackson had broken his arm early in the summer and wore a cast for most of the season. The cast came off about two weeks before we returned to school.

This explanation seemed strange but it made the most sense. Jackson broke his arm and it healed on its own. The worst had happened and he had recovered by himself. He understood that he was stronger than he thought.

The last drawings Jackson made before he returned to a regular classroom were full of muscle-bound apes.

———

*J*ackson's drawings probably contain some deeper level of psychodynamic meaning than I was aware of at the time. However, his is one story among dozens and dozens of others in which changes in the body were fundamental to changes in the learner. Many of my stories tell of learners with special needs, but that is because the stories are so dramatic and clear.

This chapter is for wondering. I wonder if experiential or "hands-on" learning is devalued because it is so tied to the work of the body. I also wonder if the role of the body in supporting learning is devalued because it is so nonlinguistic. More than anything else I wonder about the importance of the body to learning. Where would other symbol systems such as language or music be without movement? Where would *any* of the arts be without movement? The intelligences are intertwined, but I wonder if bodily-kinesthetic intelligence isn't at the root of some of them.

BEGINNING WITH THE INTELLIGENCE OF THE BODY

We start out as sensorimotor learners. Infants spend much of their time learning to control their bodies and discovering the physical world (for example, object permanence). Within a few years early language development begins to map the physical world.

There is nothing particularly wrong with this account, but it is incomplete and has led us significantly astray. The fact is that reasoning, language, self-esteem, and social competence depend a great deal on the early and *ongoing* physical exploration of the world. Historically, we have come to see the learning of the body and of the senses as strictly second-class (unless one is an athlete), having little to do with cognition except in the young child (Johnson 1987; Berman 1990; Varela, Thompson, and Rosch 1991). Gardner makes a strong argument for understanding the movement of the body as an intelligence, citing the work of mimes, athletes, and dancers as more than sequences of skills. The language Gardner uses in *Frames of Mind* to describe this intelligence is intriguing: "a sense of timing, where each bit of a sequence fits into the stream in an exquisitely placed and elegant way" (1983, p. 208). He also points out some of the ways the brain generates the bodily movements that form the basis for much of human activity, from speech to writing.

THE BODY GENERATES MEANING THROUGH THE LIFESPAN

From the first moments of life to the last, the human body seeks predictability. The body functions most smoothly when pulse, breathing, and metabolic function share a basic rhythm. In this way, internal and external changes can be registered and either attended to or ignored.

The body is tuned to make these kinds of distinctions right from the start and improves with experience and exposure to the world. It has been shown, for example, that infants as young as six months can detect the shift from a ''p'' sound to a ''b'' sound. This was measured by observing changes in rhythm as they sucked on a pacifier as sounds were presented to them (Kuhl 1980).

Classification stems from this ability to make fine distinctions. While it is unquestionably true that language plays an important role, learners continue to rely on the body for assistance. Consider how often we physically sort items into groups, even as adults. We also physically count objects and people by pointing or nodding while we count; a teacher on a field trip is doing this kind of counting almost constantly. These classification experiences are critical in the development of cognition: they allow us to organize what we know more efficiently.

A sense of time is another aspect of cognition with a strong bodily basis. From the beginning, we discern patterns. The infant, for example, begins to internalize the feeding and sleeping schedule and to anticipate time cues: the sight of a bottle means feeding time and the feel of water indicates bath time.

We organize our lives against a backdrop of schedules and routines. Waking up and going to sleep are cued by certain sights and sounds. Days are structured according to the timing of different activities. Regularity develops our internal clocks. When our bodies are in tune with external time, we begin to wake up before the alarm rings, anticipate lunch, and fall asleep at predictable times.

GETTING IN TOUCH WITH FEELINGS

Our bodies are generators of meaning. As children begin to observe and experiment with the physical world, they experience different sensations and learn to recognize gradients: hot, cold, wet, dry, red, yellow are not absolutes but points on a continuum. There are degrees of anger just as there are degrees of heat. Understanding that meaning lies on a continuum makes a learner more flexible, more able to accept different solutions, strategies, and approaches. Such learners are a lot easier to be with in the long run and are probably happier.

Understanding that we experience different feelings allows us to make practical plans to respond to those feelings. I once assessed a learner named Alex, who would clean when he was upset or distressed. He would lock himself in the bathroom and start cleaning it. If you think about it, his actions show a high degree of emotional intelligence. Talking wasn't going to help, so he did something repetitive, practical, and socially rewarded and that would calm him and allow him to get on with the day.

Alex is one of many children who do something physical to relax. I have also dealt with learners who threw tantrums and required physical handling until they calmed down. This unfortunately can become a vicious cycle: teacher and learner dance a hard dance until they are both tired out. Alex's way is certainly better, and even adults have something to learn from his example. Think about the number of people you know who do something physical to relax: yoga, walking, exercising, cleaning, taking a bath—all are physical activities. We learn to relax using our bodily-kinesthetic intelligence.

TEACHING TO THE BODY: TEACHING FROM BEHIND

Children begin to construct knowledge at a very early age. When a caregiver holds an infant from behind, the infant feels stabilized. Both can give their attention to their immediate surroundings. Together, they point and jointly focus on objects and events. The infant is learning how to pay attention. A learning dialogue develops between the caregiver and the child and as the infant reacts to the adult's direction (''What's that?''). Trust, security, and a sense of empathy grow from such powerful interactions (Affolter 1987).

Children acquire the basics of learning to learn as they begin to ask questions and respond to the teacher's focus. I have heard many teachers talk of children's difficulty in doing either. In a real way, this resembles the play-debrief-replay dialogue (see Chapter 9). The adult responds to the child's initiatives by adding focus, direction, and challenge.

As certain movements, such as waving good-bye, are ritualized, the infant starts to anticipate the next step and makes the movement without adult prompting. As the child becomes more competent the adult can move to the side. Later, as the child ''internalizes'' these movements and does them independently, the adult can be anywhere.

It is interesting to take the principle of ''teaching from behind'' both literally and metaphorically. In a literal sense, it tells teachers to be careful not to make ourselves part of the routine. If we insist that children hang up their coats every day and then stand in front of the coat hooks and point, we become part of the routine. For us to complain that little Billy

Figure 10   We teach from behind more often than we realize. Here Susan Porter, a university student, plays piano with Jonathon.

never does anything unless we keep an eye on him overlooks the fact that we have taught him to rely on us. We have created a routine without considering how to hand it over.

Teaching from behind is not only a one-on-one technique. I often sit at the side or the back of the classroom when I work with children, letting them run the class, read the schedule, or tell a story. I manage their attention through verbal reminders (but I will also physically reorient learners when the need arises). In doing so I am demonstrating how to pay attention and how to be a learning audience. The point is not to make a child pay attention but to teach inner control (Vygotsky 1978).

Beyond this, however, "teaching from behind" is a way of envisioning the relationship between teachers and students. As teachers, we stabilize, focus, and even direct children's attention, but we also have to accept and respond to the directions in which they choose to go.

ACCOMPLISHMENT

There is a deeper issue. I truly think that when an activity is over, and children know it's over, they have a sense of accomplishment. The tangible end result that marks the completion of an activity—finishing a painting, putting together a puzzle, building an Aztec temple—not only records the accomplishment, it forms a record of the brain's work, proof that there was a plan and an investment of effort. The painting or puzzle or temple becomes something children can point to and reflect upon.

Even learners with a limited symbolic capacity can and should experience this sense of physical accomplishment. When I started as a volunteer in an occupational therapy program all those years ago, I worked with a range of learners. I watched these clever professionals make adaptations to the environment so that many learners could accomplish everything from daily living activities, like eating with greater independence, to simple leisure activities. They made it possible for these individuals to be practical and to experience the simple joy of accomplishing a physical task. I also think we underestimate the degree to which developing basic bodily-kinesthetic intelligence contributes to better overall interpersonal intelligence. If you get out and play, you have more opportunities to interact. More opportunities to interact means more chances to strengthen your interpersonal intelligence and have some successes in this area. The explicit rules and structures of sports allow some children to succeed as a member of a group in ways they ordinarily would not.

I remember Stefan, a learner who was physically and especially clumsy. He could not cross the classroom without crashing and tripping over everyone and everything. It did not help his popularity. Moreover, he just could not succeed at the local game of "wall ball," much as he wanted to. Throw into the mix some significant difficulties in understanding and speaking, and it is not surprising that he'd get into fights on the playground.

For such a learner, there were obviously several other crucial goals, but everyone involved thought one of the most important was to teach him to play "wall ball." To its eternal credit, the school understood that this would require one-on-one teaching. Each day Stefan would practice going out to the wall and trying to throw the ball. Each day, an assistant would guide him from behind until he had mastered the basic motion. Eventually, he succeeded.

He received a new tennis ball (a prized commodity) and was exceedingly proud of his accomplishment. Some time later, at a new school, he mounted his treasured tennis ball in a Styrofoam cup and taped the whole thing to his desk. True, it was not the reason he was given the ball, but it was something he could look at every day. He had a good memory for things he saw, so it makes sense that this is how he would represent and value his accomplishment. We taught him from behind—literally when he learned to throw the ball and symbolically when we let him represent his accomplishment in his own way.

It was an accomplishment Stefan carried with him for years afterward. When I last spoke with him, on a street corner many years later, I hardly recognized him, but he knew me and reintroduced himself as "the boy who learned to throw a ball." It was the dividing line in his life and an important part of his life story.

RECOMMENDED READING

Ackerman, Diane. *A Natural History of the Senses.* New York: Random House, 1990.

A lively book about the five senses that mixes poetic images with fascinating facts.

Affolter, Felicie. *Perception, Interaction in Language: Interaction of Daily Living: The Root of Development.* Berlin, Heidelberg: Springer-Verlag, 1987.

This book outlines, in great detail, ways of teaching children who need to become more physically organized and coordinated. I know of no other book quite like it, but the techniques illustrated here can also be found in the literature related to the education of children with visual and physical impairments.

Wilkinson, Joyce A. *The Symbolic Dramatic Play—Literacy Connection: Whole Brain, Whole Body, Whole Learning.* Needham Heights, MA: Ginn Press, 1993.

Drama is one of those disciplines that educates the body and uses it for self-expression. The author takes pains to point out the valuable role of the body and dramatic play in learning.

11

The Form of Thinking: Aesthetics

It is only when the deepest sound from my heart meets the deepest sound coming forth from yours—it is only in this encounter that the true music begins.

KATHERINE PATERSON

The Spying Heart

Chess is new to the curriculum in the school where I teach, and the students in my class have had little exposure to it. We did some simple introductory activities about the chess pieces and how they moved. Then, late in the fall, we were able to invite a guest artist, Jane, to come and work with the children for a few weeks creating papier-mâché figures. I wanted to extend the student's knowledge of the chess pieces and give them a historical perspective, so we decided to make chess pieces.

Some degree of planning was involved. The first problem was aesthetics. We had to choose colors for the pieces (Would we have many colors or just two?). We had to decide on the height of the individual pieces. The larger they were, the harder they would be to use.

After some discussion, we agreed that the sets had to be one of two colors (students chose black and white), although metallic paint, feathers, and beads could be added for decoration. The class also decided to make the pieces as large as possible but keep them proportionate with each other: pawns could only be 15 cm high while kings could range up to 30 cm. Finally, since no one wanted to try to make a horse's head, we agreed that the knights could be just a sword if need be.

Next, the class had to master a number of techniques. The first was making the mixture for papier-mâché, which was a challenge in itself. One group's mixture was so thick, a spoon could stand straight up in it. John, speaking on behalf of many others, complained that it was "so cold we'll be the statues." In addition to these little problems, the children had to cut cardboard to the right size for a base and select rocks to add weight. Here the class discovered that heavy, flat-bottomed rocks were best, otherwise the base was wobbly ("They gotta be flat like your hand," said Ron).

They made sketches of their ideas knowing they could revise their plans as they went along. Getting the proportion of limbs and body parts right proved to be especially challenging. We took time for a lot of discussion and demonstration. When I walked past one group, I noticed that Kevin was standing atop his desk, meter stick held like a sword over Ron, while Colin kept saying, "Okay, hold still for another minute." It turned out that they were posing for an elaborate knight chess piece. We talked about the general proportions of the body—that the length of the forearm, for example, is the same as the length of the foot. This, of course, sparked a surge of contortions as children took off their shoes to check the truth of the proposition.

In the end, however, the results were impressive. It was fascinating to see how much of themselves learners could put into a project, even with all of the techniques they had to master. The rooks, based on castles, ranged from inviting, almost homelike constructions to formidable, booby-trapped fortresses. Queens looked both imperious and glamorous. (Arnold suggested that Aisha had made her queen to look like herself, which nearly caused a fight. Later, however, Aisha freely admitted that it was true: she thought she'd make a good queen.) The knights ranged from swords rising out of the ground to an action figure in full battle cry (the amount of blood and gore in evidence was something I'd neglected to negotiate in advance).

The chess pieces were to be shown in a display case, and we discussed how the display should be arranged. Should all the pawns go together? Should the pieces face each other or the viewer? Should the ones that turned out best be front and center? Several children claimed that this was the hardest work of all.

The chess piece project seemed to take forever, made a constant mess (I still shudder at the thought of papier-mâché, paint, newspaper), and took time away from other things I felt we had to cover. Still without realizing it, we had discussed symmetry and proportion in nature (rocks, human bodies), chess, the nature of mixtures, as well as castles and medieval times, just to name a few.

In the end, everything balanced out.

BEGINNING AESTHETICS

When I first read about Gardner's entry points, I felt I had a basic understanding of everything but aesthetics. I could see it as an approach for those with a strong arts perspective, but I wasn't sure how it could work in an everyday classroom. I wondered what I could do to help foster an understanding of aesthetics. If that wasn't enough, I also wondered how to get children ready to use aesthetics as an entry point. The older children could do it, but what about the younger ones?

Actually, the more I got hold of a workable sense of what aesthetics is, the easier it all became. Aesthetics is a subject for philosophers, art critics, and art educators (Ross 1984; Moore 1994). Gardner himself has referred to this issue, particularly in *Art, Mind, and Brain* (1982) and *The Arts and Human Development* (1994). It is easy to get buried in discussion without coming to a conclusion, yet in discussing the aesthetic roles involved, I have begun to understand this entry point. The chess pieces are an example. The *creators* of the pieces are the children themselves. When the children arranged them in the display case, they also became *producers,* reinterpreting their art for viewers (another example: every time you read a story, you become a producer because you give it your own unique voice).

A third role is the *audience,* all those who see the work. For the chess pieces, this included me, Jane, the artist, and everyone who visited the display cases. Audience members think about how they react to a work emotionally and what it reminds them of. It is a more personal response. Fourth, and finally, there are *critics,* who analyze the specific techniques the creator uses to communicate and how well they succeed. When Arnold suggested that Aisha was making her queen look like herself because she wanted to be a queen, he wasn't just trying to incite a riot, he was being a critic.

As Dennie Wolf (1989), a Project Zero researcher, suggests, these stances cannot be seen as separate if children are to develop an overall artistic sense. She argues that learners need to understand the strong symbiosis between the different perspectives: "Young painters need avid debate and conversation about what they see, not just an entry card to museums. Young dancers need the experience of choreographing and engaging in criticism; it is not enough to learn the steps of someone else's dance or to be able to correct the steps in line with their vision of the dance" (p. 37).

TOOLS FOR TEACHING AESTHETICS

A First Tool: An Aesthetic Triangle

Understanding these aesthetic roles helps in determining how they can be used as entry points. Borrowing from earlier chapters, there are some tools that can be reapplied here. Chambers's "likes/dislikes puzzles and patterns" (Chapter 7) can help the audience and the critic. Having a wide array of creative tools, such as paintbrushes, musical instruments, and different sized dance shoes, is essential, as are time and mentors. In addition, teaching children an aesthetic vocabulary (faster/slower, louder/softer, and so on) and the domains of art (dance: ballet, tap; music: jazz, classical, and so on) is essential if they are to develop an aesthetic sense.

Asking focus questions and giving children specific challenges can also help. Figure 11a is a kind of "aesthetics triangle" for analyzing art (if the student is the maker, some questions may be more appropriate than others). I have adapted it from a similar one used in media education (see Metropolitan Toronto School Board 1997). I show the children the triangle, which explains aesthetic roles at a glance. On occasion, we have even taken something, an audiotape, for example, and physically placed it within the triangle as we analyze and reflect on it. As a planning sheet that reminds learners of all the factors and features they might want to include in an artwork, the triangle invites creation.

In the end, however, it is the questions that are important. This list is not comprehensive, but it gets children thinking.

Figure 11a   Aesthetics triangle

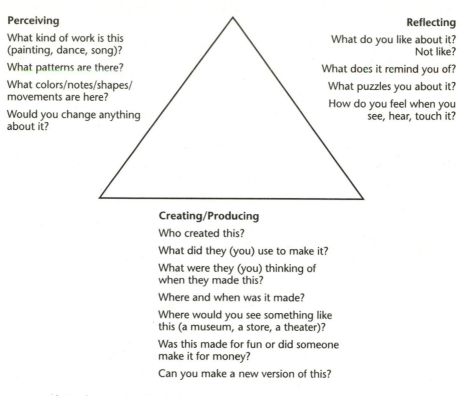

Perceiving

What kind of work is this (painting, dance, song)?

What patterns are there?

What colors/notes/shapes/ movements are here?

Would you change anything about it?

Reflecting

What do you like about it? Not like?

What does it remind you of?

What puzzles you about it?

How do you feel when you see, hear, touch it?

Creating/Producing

Who created this?

What did they (you) use to make it?

What were they (you) thinking of when they made this?

Where and when was it made?

Where would you see something like this (a museum, a store, a theater)?

Was this made for fun or did someone make it for money?

Can you make a new version of this?

A Second Tool: Sensory Material

Making papier-mâché is tricky. It can't be too wet and thin or it won't adhere. It can't be too thick or it will produce a lumpy surface. Getting the texture right is almost instinctive. It is hard to put into words.

Aisha complained. "How come you can't explain? Doesn't it say the answer in your teacher book?"

I began by saying that most things were probably on a continuum. I pointed out that hot is not the opposite of cold; they are simply points on a continuum, aspects of a larger whole. The same is true of good and bad, in and out, bright and dark. I thought this was a reasonably good on-the-spot explanation and was already planning activities in my head to further illustrate the point, when Aisha let out a wail. "Are you telling me I learned all my opposites for nothing?"

Painful as it may be to some children, it is important that they learn to think in flexible terms. Many teachers speak of learners who are "rigid" or "uncompromising," who see only black and white with no shades of gray. Others complain of students who regard their work as either good or bad. The use of descriptive language also depends on an individual's sensitivity to continua of meaning and is something many teachers complain about.

Working with papier-mâché was not in and of itself an aesthetic experience, it was a sensory experience. Many children loved it and would actually put the mixture on their arm to watch it dry. Others couldn't stand the stuff and let their friends do most of the mixing. Some noticed how cold the mixture was at first and would wait until it "warmed up," even suggesting the microwave (an interesting idea, though maybe not to the staff who had to use it later). Still, in Arnold's view, "Science is the poorer for not knowing."

In exploring the sensory world, children discover the subtleties of sensory experience. Teachers can help children notice these differences (Does it feel softer than before? Is that light too bright?). Teachers can also direct children's attention to any changes in the material and in their own bodily sensations (Are your hands getting colder? Is it drying out?). In this way, children begin to discover that they like one sensation but not another and form personal preferences.

Thus, playing in the sandbox, finger painting, playing in water, experimenting with all kinds of modeling dough, clay, and papier-mâché are intrinsically valuable activities. Such experiences extend and develop everything from vocabulary to a sense of personal identity. Furthermore, they prepare children for the kinds of distinctions needed in making aesthetic judgments and focus children's attention on the continuum of experience.

Art involves communication through symbols. Subtle distinctions between how words are said, how images are combined, or the form and sequence of musical notes may determine whether the audience understands a work as humorous or sad. The skilled artist can manipulate symbols to convey subtle distinctions in ideas or feelings. The more sophisticated an audience, the more they can perceive such nuances.

A Third Tool: Thinking on a Continuum

I discovered a little trick in a favorite book, *Literacy Through Literature*, (Johnson and Louis 1987). In response to a story, children mark one of five circles on a scale ranging, for example, from happy to sad. The authors suggest rating a character in a book on a scale like this. I wondered if the

Figure 11b   A class brainstorming session about good, bad, and ugly words.

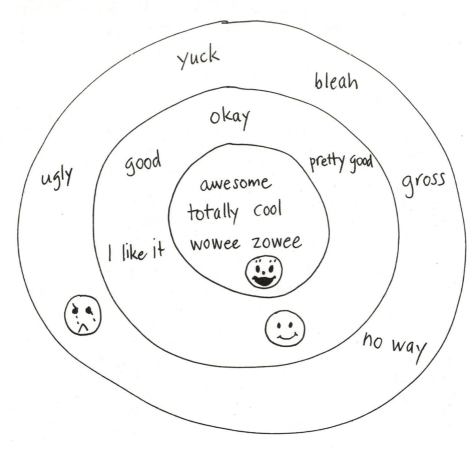

same kind of scale couldn't be used to rate more than just character attributes. For example, I used it with the grade five/six class to rate the stickiness of the papier-mâché mixture.

A different illustration from *Thinking in Education* (Lipman 1991) uses a set of concentric circles to distinguish between synonyms and antonyms: in the center circle, for example, the word *wet* and related words (*soggy, drenched,* and so on); in the outer circle, *dry* and words like *parched* and *arid;* in the middle circle, words that are not wet or dry, such as *moist, damp,* and the like.

Figure 11b combines these two visual frameworks in a diagram I have used with my kindergarten class. The children respond to a book, a snack, a television show, a piece of music, or whatever we are discussing by pointing to the center, middle, or outer ring. I have also found it helpful to let children actually draw the concentric circles in addition to brainstorming vocabulary words.

This abstract activity may take a while for kindergarten children to understand, but once they do, they begin to see that meaning lies along a continuum. It is then much easier to teach comparative vocabulary (*er* and *est* endings) and to introduce the idea that there can be many words for the same thing.

These sorts of illustrations helped the students in the grade six class to understand that even papier-mâché could involve continuums of meaning (softer to firmer, wetter to dryer, colder to warmer), and it became part of the follow-up activities for making chess pieces. However, as Arnold understood, it could lead to scientific investigation of sensory material. I once had an enrichment class investigate different types of modeling dough and report back on which they judged best in terms of durability, smell, and overall appeal. (Calling sensory investigations "science" allows you to play with the sensory components throughout the grades.) This approach does have a few perils. My principal walked in, which he does a few times during the school year, just as one group was testing the "baseballness" of the dough they'd made by pitching it across the room. I assured him it was all in the name of science.

Another way to give children a sense of continuum is to experiment with elements in one symbol system. One good art demonstration involves gradations of color. I take either black or white and mix it in various quantities with another color to produce different shades and tints of that color. In music, we play a scale on different instruments or vary the volume and speed of our singing. In gym, we practice skills in slow and fast motion replays. Aesthetics need not be an arid subject. It should be a messy, "get your hands dirty" activity that builds complex thinking through sensory experience.

Pattern and Aesthetics

A sense of pattern allows learners to create or perceive relationships among a set of symbols. Patterns can also illustrate terms like *harmony, symmetry,* and *balance,* which are essential to a sense of aesthetics. Pattern is a common theme in many primary classrooms since it informs so many areas of knowledge. For teachers who might think they don't have the time for an aesthetic entry point, consider some of the following anecdotes.

Paulo wanted my attention but waited as patiently as he could while I read Gerald McDermott's *Zomo the Rabbit: A Trickster Tale from West Africa* to Shaniqua.

The story, in brief, involves a rabbit named Zomo, who is given three tasks by the sky god. I had read the book to the class about a dozen times, discussed the symmetry in its illustrations, and explored with the class some of the patterns within the story. I felt in command as I began to talk with Shaniqua.

Paulo could not contain himself as I slipped past what he called the "most important page." "Oh," I said, "tell me what's important on this page."

"You know," he said. "The sky god's clothes have all the pictures of the jobs that Zomo has to do." Sure enough, there were little icons that clearly represented each of the tasks.

"Don't tell me you didn't see those," he said. "It tells you what's going to happen before it happens."

Paulo understood the overall pattern of the book well enough to know the outline of events, and because he did, he was able to assume the role of critic and identify subtle visual clues to the story. Beyond responding to the pattern aesthetically, Paulo also used it to enter the story.

I don't attempt to make pattern a special theme or topic. I want it to be a part of the daily conversation, one of the tools of thinking. Even the most mundane object can be the subject of pattern investigation. For example, one rainy day Faiza brought an umbrella to school. I pointed out a sun, a moon, a smaller sun, a girl, and a jug of milk all in a row on the umbrella. I invite Faiza to continue "reading" the pictures, and eventually she and a few others noticed a pattern. Other umbrellas, raincoats, and boots were enthusiastically (and soggily) investigated for more patterns. Many children ended up wet and far more aware of the aesthetics of rain gear.

As the year advances, children begin to use this emerging aesthetic sense to enter the world at large. Discussions about pattern move across symbol systems and become more precise. There are higher notes and lower notes on the piano; then someone demonstrates the pattern of C keys along the keyboard. Shapes begin to acquire names. Descriptions add color and size and quantity ("It's a bunch of fat red lines"). Emotions enter in: "I like those pedal sounds," says Kenya pushing the piano pedals with her feet while her friend plays the keys. The children start separating tapes into

Figure 11c   Micheal made up a game about symmetry: Find the parts on one side of the picture that are not the same as those on the other side.

favorite and less favorite piles and then into genres ("That's too much like country"; "That's got fast songs on it"). We discovered symmetry as we used makeup on faces and later as children drew pictures featuring symmetry.

I'll give the last word to Paulo. When he made his observation of the story of Zomo, I rallied as best as I could and asked, "Who put those symbols there?" After a moment of back and forth, he replied, "The person who made the pictures. They wanted you to know, if you were paying attention, that is."

An Aesthetic Understanding of a Computer

As befits a chapter about aesthetics, I have used a triangle to elicit understanding of aesthetics. It seemed to me that young children could also understand the ideas contained in the triangle if they were presented in the right way. Over the last number of years, I have experimented with different versions of this triangle, which can be used to analyze and to create.

The computers in our classroom are always on. Eventually children use them independently and I can come and go, offering advice. A simple little math computer game generated much excitement when the children discovered that a little icon frowned for a second when they gave a wrong answer. The game had been in use for a long time, and I never did figure out who made this discovery.

It was a big hit. Pictures and physical imitations of unsmiling faces erupted everywhere. The children dreamed up new computer screens with features like buzzers and screaming heads to tell you when you were right or wrong. Since we were also talking about shapes at the time, someone connected a crescent shape with the smiling and unsmiling face, which is why (I think) the face came to be called a "banana face."

The creators of the program had put in that face to indicate a wrong answer. What they could not have anticipated was the response of the class to this bit of programming. The children found it hilarious. They made mistakes again and again just to see the face frown. When we discussed the situation, Micheal said, "It's supposed to make you feel bad 'cause you maked a mistake but it doesn't. It's just funny." At five, they understood the difference between what someone intended and what they in fact felt.

To use aesthetics as an entry point into media, take a feature like a sound, an image, or a movement. Then look at some simple collectible (there is always something) for aesthetic patterns (it can be a trading card, a toy from a fast food restaurant, the latest plaything, even the packaging from these products). Is it always glossy? How big is it? What shape is it? What does it remind you of? Which ones are the best? What feature makes these the best? Then elicit connections between these features and how they make you feel. The children realize that the frowning face in the computer game actually made them happy. And what child doesn't know that darkness and shadow are associated with scary situations? I have also heard a child of three chant "The cars gonna crash, the music is fast" over and over when the music reached a crescendo.

Other questions focus on the intentions of the designer: Who made the scary show? When do you see it? How did it scare you? What commercials did they use? This sounds difficult, but Paulo, for example, understood who made the pictures in the Zomo picture book and why. Micheal identified the real intentions of the designers of the computer game.

The easiest way for children to understand this simple analytical framework is to experience it. Making new pictures for the computer program is one example, but it can also be applied to those annoying fads that hit your classroom.

A few years ago, when Pogs—small, round, collectibles used for a simple game—were all the rage, my grade three/four class began to make them. That prompted students to look at what made a "good" pog—bright colors, a ghoulish image, a shiny surface, and most of all, a unique "collectible" design.

"It's like kids' money," Nelson said. I marveled at the truth of this and wondered if the people who made the product knew that it was like kids' money. If that wasn't enough, Adrian said, "Holding something scary means you are strong." His comment reminded me of all the new horror books and wonder if that wasn't their real appeal. Listening to them I learned more than I thought I could about a silly product.

Using All Sides of Aesthetics to Understand Dance

We can all be critics. As Aidan Chambers argues, children are far more capable than we think of digging into an author's intentions, use of symbols, and the feelings and meanings a work evokes (1996). Chambers's framework invites children to comment on the aesthetics of fiction. Children discuss patterns, ponder the pieces of a story, and think about what an author might mean. Although Chambers uses his approach with literature, a form of verbal art, many picture books are substantial visual works of art in their own right. Many also play with the rhythms and forms of language in ways that are poetic or musical. Thus, in talking about a picture book, we have already touched on several aesthetic dimensions. I have tried to extend this aesthetic framework. One day, as part of the "dancing year," we watched short video clips of tap dancing and street dancing. The children's response was immediate and surprising: they were more taken with the tap dancing.

"I like the noise the feet make."

"I like the way they stand straight."

"I like the music—it's so fast."

They watched the video dozens of times during the week that followed. They began to identify with certain dancers ("I'm that guy"; "I'm her—look at how fast her feet go"). They listened intently as Darcia demonstrated shoes for Flamenco and tap, which sent them off on a new round of discussions about which sound they preferred.

They sprang into action and created a little theater out of the classroom entranceway. They tried on Darcia's tap shoes and to my surprise got some sound out of them, which was no mean feat, considering that they were adult shoes. Their interest went on so long, we actually went out and purchased four cheap pairs of running shoes and put real taps on them. The first few times children tried out the shoes, the energy they invested was the most intense I have ever seen. They began to make up little dances, again using the entranceway as a stage and practiced moves they had seen. John, on his first day with the tap shoes, actually make a 360-degree turn and then did the splits.

Entering Wider Fields of Knowledge Through Aesthetics

In very simple ways, children were using the aesthetics of dance movement to enter other realms. Aside from learning dance terminology, some children also became interested in what 360 degrees meant. Then we looked at 180 degrees, a more manageable turn for most. Later, they went for 90 degrees.

The investigations entered into other areas. The children looked at shoes as never before. "How come some shoes is soft in the heel and not others?" asked Karla. "Can you make tap shoes with any metal? Does it gotta be special?" asked Funsho, obviously making plans. Darien asked, "How come everyone likes those clicking noises so much? Usually I hate noisy shoes." This led some to consider the sounds in the world around them and how they were made.

Finally, they began to notice patterns: all dance involves moving the feet, all dance involves music. Tap dancing seemed to need fast, "jumpy" music, someone said. Where does that music come from? Where is that on the map [globe]? What dance comes from Nigeria [where the child was from]? And finally, why are there so many dances? Who makes up dances?

One day, just when I thought the learning had finally plateaued, I saw Shaniqua sitting quietly at a table. She had carefully laid out a few markers and was singing to herself as she drew. I couldn't figure out what she was making, so I finally stopped and asked.

"A map of the people dancing. This is some people here and this is some people there. They dancing. The yellow [referring to yellow dots on the page] go this way." Stunned, I realized she had made a map of the kind

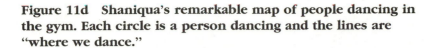

Figure 11d   Shaniqua's remarkable map of people dancing in the gym. Each circle is a person dancing and the lines are "where we dance."

of dance we had done in the gym and appeared to be making plans for other dances.

"I got dancing in my brain," Shaniqua said.

I could only agree.

CREATORS AND AUDIENCES: THE AESTHETICS OF SAND

In the popular mind, artists are idiosyncratic individuals who hear and see things in ways different from the rest of us. This is doubtless an overgeneralization—but then there was Alvin.

I met him many years ago as part of an assessment I was to do with him. We were in the gym with his grade four classmates. On feeling the grittiness of the gym floor, Alvin began to recall all of the times he had felt that kind of grittiness before. You never knew where Alvin was going to go with a subject. It took the better part of three mornings of conversation to establish that what Alvin was talking about was grittiness. In that time we covered trips to Hawaii (beaches), the feel of the exterior of his apartment building (brick), anthills (and everything about ants, which I guess he liked because of the feel of anthills), the face of any male because of the stubble (he had an uncle who never shaved).

I remember these conversations clearly because of the tremendous feeling of anxiety I had as we swooped from one topic to another. Alvin wasn't the slightest bit perturbed: it all made sense to him. I wished I had known more debriefing strategies back then, but it probably wouldn't have made any difference. What I did was listen. I was an audience learning about the aesthetics of sand. In fact, it was the anthills that finally cued me that this was about sand. "Sand!" I shouted. "You like talking about sand and everything that feels like sand."

"I guess so," he said. "I never think about that before." His smile was the smile of someone who'd been understood.

Indeed, once I got a grip on the pattern it was relatively easy to follow Alvin's train of thought. It was also possible to understand some of his unusual behavior, such as putting sand and glue over anything he wrote. He didn't look quite so odd. I'd love to be able to say what happened to him but he moved far away. My assessment report included recommendations for working with clay, brainstorming synonyms for *gritty,* and poetry followed him.

One day, about a year and a half later, I received a curious piece of mail. It was from a teacher in another part of the country who thought I'd like to know what Alvin was doing. The letter said little more than that, but enclosed were photographs of two pieces of artwork. The first was a jar filled with colored sand. The second was an elaborate collage of different shades of sand, small rocks and other small elements entitled *At the Beach.*

The appreciation of subtle distinctions ranges across the intelligences. In a real way, Alvin was drawn to the aesthetic aspects of grit, beginning with its feel. However, he also had strong visual memory ("The best anthill I ever see . . .") that would be meaningless to anyone else. As idiosyncratic as some people's aesthetics may be, they may qualify for that label because of the subtlety of the distinctions these individuals perceive and create. At some very deep level, Alvin displayed an almost refined sense of what was beautiful. A witness to his passion, I have always been a little more aware of the texture of dirt.

When I met him, he was still learning about the symbols of his chosen passion. He had not yet become a creator in any sense we recognized, though I wonder what would have happened if we had let him mark up his writing a little more with sand and glue.

At the time, I had no sense of an entry point but he clearly did. His attention ran to beaches, anthills, beards, and building materials. Just think of the ones he might have gone on to cover if the passion stayed with him—deserts, soils, erosion.

In a similar way, there are people who appreciate a dance, a painting, or a piece of music the rest of us are hard put to equal. But as an audience to that passion, we can learn to make similar distinctions. This perspective is important because those who become deeply engaged in certain aesthetics can seem odd to us. Learners with autism can be deeply engaged by everything from the twirling motion of a piece of string, to the rhythm of a piece of music, to the alphabet. We don't see, hear, or feel as they might. I want to argue, however, that such learners may also belong on the continuum with those "artistic" people we know who also see, hear, and feel in different ways. Artistic individuals may use more conventional aesthetics and may even clearly communicate some of their aesthetic understanding to nonartists through language. However, all learners need appreciation and understanding of their passion and perhaps encouragement. Yet I wonder how often we miss the ways in which such learners enter the world aesthetically.

I think about it every time I go the beach.

RECOMMENDED READING

Picture Books

McDermott, Gerald. *Zomo the Rabbit: A Trickster Tale from West Africa.* New York: Harcourt Brace, 1992.

This is the version of the story that struck Paulo as so interesting. The illustrations are works of art.

Seuss, Dr. *My Many Colored Days.* Illus. Steve Johnson and Lou Fancher. New York: Random House, 1996.

A marvelous book that links colors and feelings. I have had some luck in getting young children to begin to connect feeling with color and have been intrigued at the different colors children relate to emotions.

Williams, Helen. *Stories in Art.* Brookfield, CT. Milbrook Press, 1991.

> It was hard to decide whether this belongs with stories or aesthetics. A simple little picture book, it is here because it contains so much about how an artist uses technique to tell a story. Highly recommended.

Yenawine, Philip. *Lines.* New York: Delacorte Press with The Museum of Modern Art, 1991.

————. *Stories.* New York: Delacorte Press with The Museum of Modern Art, 1991.

————. *Shapes.* New York: Delacorte Press with The Museum of Modern Art, 1991.

> Each book includes a series of reproductions of paintings from various eras. I have found them useful in introducing children to famous artists, style, and technique. Most interesting, these books lend themselves to simple questions about the relationship between technique and audience response.

Reference Books

Gardner, Howard. *Artful Scribbles: The Significance of Children's Drawings.* New York. Basic Books, 1980.

> A basic work in which Gardner discusses aesthetics and young children's conceptions of art. He also goes onto to examine how children's art and concepts about art change over the course of childhood. There are many examples of children's drawings throughout the book. While I'm not sure that my own experience supports everything he has to say, it is very readable and engaging.

Joyce, Mary. *First Steps in Teaching Creative Dance to Children.* 3rd. ed. Mountain View, CA: Mayfield, 1994.

> Darcia Isenor rates this a four-star book, and that's good enough for me.

Yardley, Alice. *Senses and Sensitivity.* Toronto: Rubicon Publishing, 1988.

> This is a classic, a must-have, must-read book. Now I no longer look at anything in quite the same way. It is one of a series of excellent books by this amazing educator, who was, and still is, years ahead of her time. (See References for additional titles.)

12

Interlude: Wondering About Metaphor and Thinking

Metaphors are figures of speech in which the literal meaning of words is transformed by application to a new, less literal context: for example, screaming headlines or lateral thinking. Although we use them every day, I suspect most of us pay little attention to them. I think my own interest in metaphor was sparked some years ago when I had to conduct a formal assessment of someone who did not want to be formally assessed. Giving formal tests in language has never been one of my favorite activities, but I generally learn something in the process of giving one. For Ryan, however, taking formal tests has probably never been one of his favorite things, particularly where language is concerned. Tremendously bright in many ways, he was very delayed overall in language. The question of how delayed was the reason for the assessment.

In such contexts, the goal is to let the child set the pace while still getting through the basic tasks. I came up with a variation for Ryan by allowing him free access to sweet, chewy candies, which I referred to as ''smart pills.'' He thought this was amusing and began to help himself whenever he needed a break. He particularly liked some shiny green ones he called "sparkly smart pills." He insisted that they sparkled and indeed, they were a neon green that did sparkle a bit when held up to the light.

We continued for a while and we were getting through all the required tasks when, inevitably, the green candies were almost gone. Staring woefully at the last one, Ryan declared, "I can't do more."

"How come?" I asked.

"No more sparkly greens. They make me think sparkly."

There was no talking him into finishing until I got more sparkly candies. As a result, it didn't quite register at the time that this child, with significant difficulties in expressing himself, had not only referred to his cognition but had done so in a metaphoric image.

I had always thought metaphors were for poets or adults, not children with language difficulties. Was Ryan's statement an accident, a "mis-statement"? It didn't strike me that way, but I didn't think about it too much. It didn't seem central to the assessment or to Ryan's overall thinking. Over the years, of course, I have been reminded many times of just how "unsparkly" my own thinking was. The fact is that the role of metaphor in the development of thinking has inspired serious discussion (Ortony 1993).

DEVELOPMENT OF METAPHOR

Ellen Winner (1988) has written a comprehensive survey of the development of metaphor and irony in young children. Even young children, she found, can process metaphor. When they did not understand, it was more often because they didn't have enough general knowledge of the world than a problem with language. Gardner, who is married to Winner, has collaborated with her on the subject of metaphoric development (1993). Early use of metaphor, Winner notes, is based on the sensory and play experiences of young children, which they extend into metaphor, calling a red balloon an apple, for example. I have heard young children compare eating a peppery snack to making their mouths go on fire, announce that a mud puddle was like "dirt crying his eyes out," and speak of a toy frog that got wet as being "slippery like your tongue."

Further support for the idea that bodily experience is a prime source of metaphor can be found in the work of a pair of linguists, Mark Johnson and George Lakoff (Lakoff and Johnson 1980; Lakoff 1987; Johnson 1987, 1993). They argue that metaphoric knowledge is derived from our bodily experience of the world. So, for example, our actual experiences with putting things into containers leads to metaphors such as "putting a lid on something," "feeling trapped," "getting into an activity." They propose that early and ongoing sensory experiences enrich our intelligences in ways we are not aware of and influence the logic of how we think—and feel—in profound ways. Consider the experience of being enclosed in a box or a large block construction. It has a distinct feel that most of us can probably conjure up right now, and whether the resulting feeling is "boxed in" or secure depends on past experiences with this sensation.

Saying one is "boxed in" is more than a pun. It is something learned from the experience of being in containers, playing with containers, building with containers, and noticing the effects of containers on people and objects. The bodily experience sets up the metaphor, and without that kind of experience, the metaphor would not exist. This is worth bearing in mind the next time anyone questions the sensory and play-based aspects of a program.

METAPHOR AND THINKING

Winner (1988) cites evidence that metaphor may lay the groundwork for the use of analogy, itself a critical thinking skill. More broadly, as Winner says, "Metaphor helps us to clarify, to explain, to reveal" (p. 107). It helps us to see with new eyes, to speak new languages, and to dance the dance of thinking.

Lakoff and Johnson have argued that metaphor is in fact the *primary* basis for the construction and the constraint of imagination. They give numerous examples in which apparently illogical decision making is accounted for far better by examining the underlying metaphors. Lakoff and Johnson argue that knowledge, logic, and thinking are subjective rather than objective processes. In *The Body in the Mind* Johnson (1987) looks at how Hans Selye, a physician, came up with his model of stress and human health. Previous theories viewed the body as a mechanistic machine in which specific "parts" broke down. But Selye noticed the more general, nonspecific effects of stress. He revised the metaphoric framework from a mechanistic to a more homeostatic, organic model. In this model, the body fights to self-regulate and maintain balance, a key metaphor and the organizing concept in Selye's study of stress in human life.

This is a good example of approaching a subject through an aesthetic entry point. Oddly, considering that Gardner has done a great deal of research on metaphor (see Winner and Gardner 1993), I couldn't find any mention in general of the role of symbol systems in the development of metaphor (although I might have seen it and not perceived its significance). Music, for example, gives us the concepts of "harmony" and "tone." Consider how often these words are used metaphorically: "living in harmony," "toning down a piece of writing." Think of some of the images that arise in other symbol systems: in visual-spatial, "perspective," "point of view," "dimension"—(and "sparkly"); in movement, concepts of "balance," "force," and "strength." This kind of use is also relevant to a discussion of entry points. Gardner mentions that an aesthetic entry point may go as far as looking at "balance of political forces" (1991, p. 246), clearly implying he regards metaphoric applications of entry points as valid.

The evidence that metaphor and related poetic devices actually form a powerful cognitive process comes from many directions besides Lakoff, Johnson, and Winner. David Bohm, a famous theoretical physicist, wrote a number of books toward the end of his life on the nature of scientific thought and creativity. Among them was one called *Science, Order and Creativity* (1987), written with F. David Peat, in which they also argue that metaphor is an essential component in the development of scientific knowledge and insight. They also bemoan the fact that modern science and scientists have devalued the kinds of thinking necessary for creativity. What is most interesting are the examples of scientific discovery that clearly resulted from use of metaphor (such as advances in concepts of wave/particle theory).

Metaphors also play a powerful role in the study of human thought. Pribram (1990), notes of the extensive use of metaphor and analogy in neuroscience. Bruner and Feldman (1990) illustrate the use of metaphors in all sorts of talk about consciousness and cognition: we speak of "heightening awareness," "concentrating on an idea," "removing a distraction." Metaphor is implicated in the study of psychology (Leary 1990), moral development (Johnson 1993), scientific discovery (Bohm and Peat 1987), and thinking in general (Ortony 1993).

For our purposes, however, metaphor is important because of the role it plays in our classrooms. It becomes easy to see how often we describe our thinking and feeling through metaphor. It's as if metaphor becomes the currency through which we talk about our thoughts and feelings.

METAPHORS ABOUT TEACHING AND THINKING

In his book *Beginning with Ourselves: In Practice, Theory, and Human Affairs,* David Hunt (1987) discusses the role of metaphor in teaching. He describes his work with teachers around some of the metaphors they use to describe their thinking. For me, this "hit a little closer to home," and when I talked with teachers I started to listen harder. Sure enough, I hear phrases like "I feel like I'm talking to a brick wall" and "go with the flow of the classroom" all the time.

Consider how often we describe our thinking metaphorically. "Being stuck" at a "certain point" in a problem is based on the idea that the problem is a kind of a journey or pathway. Problem solving is a "step-by-step" approach. We talk of "constructing knowledge," of "bridges" between what children know in one situation and what we want them to understand in another. Data "pile up," children's learning is "scaffolded," language is a "tool," we get "information overload" and "burn out."

Children too speak in metaphors. Ryan talked of his sparkly thinking, but I have also seen and heard young children make lightbulb noises and gestures when they had an idea. I think they get this gesture from the media, but they understand that having an idea is like having a light come on. (And countless teachers have encoded an "aha" moment for children by saying "the light came on" or "you see the light.")

A social worker once mentioned to me that one could get children to articulate a range of feelings by asking, "What is the weather like inside— sunny, warm, cold, cloudy, rainy?" This has proven a wonderful technique. Children as young as five have responded with indications of their feelings when other ways have not succeeded. One particularly empathetic girl discussed what she thought the weather was like *inside me* whenever she saw me. Some children really take off and begin to speak of the weather inside their brains. Amy once said she had a "snowstorm" in her brain when she wished to convey that she had no thoughts. I was mystified for a moment and then asked, "Because everything is stuck?" and she nodded vigorously.

For me, storytelling remains the most powerful vehicle for metaphor. In "Viewpoints: Metaphors and Monsters—Children's Storytelling" Pickering and Attridge (1990) state that "Metaphor takes language beyond being the support for literal communication and mere rationality. Instead, they become expressive and creative. Because of this, metaphor and other forms of figurative language have an important role in the generative processes which underlie narrative" (p. 415). They go on to explain the work of Giambattista Vico, an eighteenth-century philosopher who considered metaphor the very essence of human reasoning, and from there to a survey of psychoanalytic theorists such as Freud, Jung, and Melanie Klein.

I have heard some remarkable narratives in which metaphor served as the vehicle for powerful, emotionally charged material. Even now, it is hard for me to shake the image of a boy in one of my classes who dreamed that he was stopping hockey shots made by famous hockey players. The dream would end with him stopping the puck—which then got up on legs and ran past him. When he looked, he saw that it had the face of his father.

Or the story another boy told of an emerald ring that kept coming back in different forms—an emerald box, an emerald coin—to haunt a group of people. With each return it brought more bad luck. The family kept trying to get rid of it but it kept coming back. This story riveted my grade six class and I asked the boy's mother when she dropped by the school if she had any guesses about its meaning. But she was as puzzled as I was. A week or so later, she returned with a slightly shaken look. She said that a long lost and scary relative had an emerald ring.

In the classroom, metaphors show up everywhere—in storytelling, poetry, drama, painting, gym lessons, computer work, math lessons. The case for "sparkly" thinking is much more certain than I once thought.

RECOMMENDED READING

Bohm, David, and F. David Peat. *Science, Order and Creativity.* Toronto: Bantam Books, 1987.

Some excellent thoughts on the use of metaphor in science and on the role of creativity in scientific discovery. It is a book for those interested in more philosophical aspects of metaphors.

Lakoff, George, and Mark Johnson. *Metaphors We Live By.* Chicago: University of Chicago Press, 1980.

Easily the most accessible book by this pair. It gives a fine overview and probably offers as much insight into conversations with other adults or political rhetoric as it does into day-to-day classroom practice.

Pickering, John, and Steve Attridge. "Viewpoints: Metaphors and Monsters—Children's Storytelling." *Research in the Teaching of English,* 24 (1990): 415–440.

A wide-ranging article that encompasses children's stories, philosophy, psychodynamic theory, and metaphor. I find it a bit of a wild ride but in the end it makes the simple point that children are up to far more than we imagine when they tell a story.

Winner, Ellen. *The Point of Words: Children's Understanding of Metaphor and Irony.* Cambridge, MA: Harvard University Press, 1988.

A solid, well-written overview of the subject. You don't need a linguistics background to read it, but it does discuss issues that may be outside the interest of the average classroom teacher. Still, this may be the book to help you understand some of the fascinating complexity of language development.

13

Tales of Thinking: Storytelling

Put your play into formal narratives, and I will help you and your classmates listen to one another. In this way you will build a literature of images and themes, of beginnings and endings, of references and allusions. You must invent your own literature if you are to connect your ideas to the ideas of others.

Vivian Gussin Paley

The Boy Who Would Be a Helicopter: The Uses of Storytelling in the Classroom

---

In Toronto, where I live, there is a large storytelling community, and I found my way to a corner of it and learned to tell stories. We would consider the claim that the audience listening to the story is as important as the teller telling it. There is a saying, "Three golden apples fell from heaven, one for the teller, one for the listener, and one for the one who heard." I wondered exactly what that meant. It sounded right in some way, but I couldn't connect it to anything I knew. One day, and there always is a "one day" in any story, I found out when I went to a grade three classroom.

I hadn't visited that classroom to tell stories in long time, probably a year. It was well set up for storytelling. There was a storyteller's chair, a ritual of selected children lighting candles, a teacher (Peter Gillis again) who told stories every day, a whole class of grade four/five students who had learned to tell stories themselves, and even a tradition of bringing stuffed animals to sit with.

The air in the room almost crackled with anticipation. This audience would make the day's stories come alive. I knew that before I even sat down. I told a few stories I was pretty sure that they had not heard, and then a couple of others I knew they liked. The students enjoyed them all, some more than others. Some were personal favorites and others were "pleasant diversions." With each story, however, they knew and I knew the final story was coming. I didn't tell them what it was and they didn't ask, but we all knew.

It is a story I have only heard. I have never seen it in a book and no one quite remembers where it came from. This is unusual in a large storytelling community, where people are generous with their sources for stories or where they can be found. It is a story about a boy, a very lazy boy, named Jack. Lazy as he is, he wanders off into the woods, where he falls asleep. He wakes up wet from the rain and goes to look for a place to dry off. What happens next is that he meets an old woman, who tells him to take off his wet clothes, one by one, until he is huddling under some sheets. Then she tells him to take off his skin . . .

This is the barest outline of the story, and I've left out all the rhythmic, repetitive, almost hypnotic qualities as well as the surprise ending. (If anyone knows where it came from, I'd love to hear. By now, I suspect, the story has been so modified by each teller it has a true folktale flavor and the original may be unrecognizable.)

This is the story they wanted, the creepiest one I know. The class had heard it exactly once the year before. This time, when I began, something strange happened: there was a murmuring in the audience. As I kept talking, I realized that they were telling the story with me, every word, every terrible turn. Having heard it once, they remembered it and had waited for this moment to make it come alive again. I told it as they huddled together, they told it, we told it to each other.

One for the teller, one for the audience, and one for the one who heard.

———

 t is time we get serious about the importance of narrative (spoken or written, fictional or autobiographical) in the classroom. Narrative is perhaps the most durable of all oral forms, and if there has been one constant in an enormous number of fields over the last twenty years, it is the role of narrative in social, emotional, and cognitive development. As a technique for understanding it adapts to investigation of all sorts of subjects (Polkinghorne 1988). There are powerful data to support the notion that narrative (or stories as one form of narrative) is a primal force in our lives. The data emerge from every perspective—cognitive development (Egan 1986; Bruner 1986, 1990), language and literacy development (Barton and Booth 1990; Duchan 1991; Heath 1983; Meek 1991; Nelson 1989; Wells 1986; Westby 1985, 1988), personal and professional development (Witherall and Noddings 1991), and theories about the very nature and development of the self (Bruner and Weisser 1991).

Obviously stories are also a way of thinking in their own right as well as an entry point to many subjects. Like other entry points, stories open up the worlds of cognition and personal identity. Just as obviously, however, learning to create, perform, and respond to stories relies on a strong foundation of skills. Stories draw on all the intelligences: they are highly linguistic, but they also have elements of sequence, organization, character, and aesthetics. They contain ethical dilemmas, problem solving, humor, and metaphor. They embed information about places, people, and things.

Among Gardner's entry points, the use of stories is most familiar to me and probably to other teachers, so that finding something new to say is difficult. After all, most teachers have used a story to introduce or extend a topic. Here, I want to demonstrate tools for stories, some reasons for telling them, and some of the ways I have used stories with learners.

TOOLS FOR STORIES

Time for Reflection

In Peter Gillis's grade three/four class, where we told the scary story to each other, several rituals marked the specialness of stories: a storytelling area, a stone to hold when telling a story, and a period of debriefing afterward, which used likes, dislikes, puzzles, and patterns. Their teacher told stories, guests told stories, and of course, students read stories.

But the greatest tool of all was the gift of time.

It is an interesting phenomenon that even young children recognize how precious a commodity time is in the contemporary world. By devoting time to stories, we tell learners how much we value stories. In a practical sense, children need uninterrupted time for reading. Over the years I've tried to schedule such reading time for first thing in the morning. In some instances, I've even paired storybooks with a breakfast program or hot chocolate.

Storytelling is further helped by comfortable spaces, which suggest slowing down to ponder and savor a story. In Peter's classroom, there is a comfortable old couch. When it is time for stories, his students sit cozily with stuffed animals to keep them company. The couch enhances the "time-out for listening" mood.

That lesson has stayed with me. When people visit our classroom, they inevitably come to the book corner, an alcove furnished with small, comfortable chairs and a sofa, surrounded by plants and stuffed animals, and stacked with all kinds of books. It doesn't simply invite reading, it begs for it.

Storytime also should include hearing stories read aloud in large groups, in small groups, and most of all one to one. I invite adult volunteers and older students to the classroom to read, and children are encouraged to take books home. Stories mean books and more books. Even picture books can touch on all kinds of subjects—philosophy, human nature, and the natural world. There are stories about mathematics and mathematicians, music and musicians, painting and painters. There are even stories about stories. Every intelligence can be found somewhere in a story (see the Recommended Reading sections of Chapters 7, 9, 11, 13, and 15).

When they have heard a story or read a book, children and teachers need time to discuss, reread, and consider the work. Individual conversations about what books are favorites also take time. Graphing activities in which the entire class records favorite books or genres or authors—these are all part of learning about yourself through stories.

I'm always intrigued by watching kindergarten children march picture books up to the piano, somehow balance them on the piano, and then make up a song about the book. Just the other day I heard Darita improvising, "Oh the cat in the hat, he's a bad cat, don't listen to him!" while banging on the drum.

Nicolas, who spent an entire year avoiding any kind of painting, turned up this fall retelling the story of Noah's Ark. One day he painted an elaborate picture of a scene from the story. Weeks later, he painted another picture of the same scene, but with much more efficiency, cleaner lines, and a better sense of balance. He informed me that it was "the real picture from the story."

The story of "The Boy Who Cried Wolf" inspires an immediate reenactment in the dancing class, involving what appear to be a pack of wolves and one or two sheep. Later, children turn to making large block houses that can be knocked down as they act out the story of "The Three Little Pigs." When children have the opportunity to respond to a story in a personal way, they discover new interests. Darita, for example, became interested in tricks, Nicolas in Bible stories and later the ocean, and the whole class in wolves.

All it took was time.

Finding a Voice

These are some of the methods I know for teaching children about the concept of story. Many will already be familiar to most teachers; however, two related tools, spoken storytelling and storyboards, are still not that widespread in some areas. Telling stories is not essential. Many teachers don't, yet they have marvelous programs that emphasize the development of narrative. Still, spoken storytelling offers riches I haven't discovered in other places.

I can vividly remember a storyboard made by Chris, a grade four student. It was crumpled and smudged, with little pencil drawings. The drawings, which were intended to outline the sequence of the story, seemed barely distinguishable from one another. Yet Chris, who was not terribly articulate or confident when speaking, had used this little piece of paper to practice a section of a story that he was to tell as part of a group.

To gain practical experience in storytelling, the class divided up into groups, and each group picked a simple story to tell. They met together and practiced. When they were ready, each group told its story. Standing up in front of their classmates, the children were nervous. I was nervous. Chris looked really nervous, but clutching that piece of paper, he told his part of the story. The words came slowly and haltingly, but they came, and in a short time he had finished.

When I asked how he felt all he said was "I could hear my voice telling the story. I could say it easier next time."

In school, particularly in the early grades, stories erupt as soon as children come through the door. We scarcely have the time to absorb all the overlapping stories children are telling. I also know many teachers who tell a great story in the staffroom, so it strikes me as odd that telling a story for a group is so difficult. In part, it is the anxiety of performing before others, but a more important factor is that telling a well-crafted story from beginning to end takes considerable skill and practice. At the same time, traditional oral/aural storytelling now competes with visual modes, such as print and electronic media.

I am not against these forms of storytelling, but I strongly believe that narrative begins in the living voice. Learning to tell stories reinforces the process of learning to write them. Children can experiment more quickly than if they were written. And they discover different ways of constructing stories and achieving dramatic or comic effects.

Making Stories Visible

Perhaps the best thing I discovered when I started to tell stories was the storyboard. This is a simple graphic organizer that looks like cartoon strip panels. These panels contain very simple illustrations representing key points in a story and serve as a way to remember the key points (see, for example, Pehrsson and Robinson 1985).

The storyboard idea has worked for a large number of children, although it is important to begin by modeling the storyboard idea on the chalkboard a few times. It is also critical to make sure children understand that the drawings should be at the stick figure level so they do not get too involved in portraying a figure or scene perfectly. They should sketch just enough to help them remember (see Faiza's example in Figure 13).

I have been intrigued by how little detail is needed to help learners remember a story. Some children, like Chris, used crumpled pieces of paper with what appear to be the sketchiest of drawings, yet, these drawings are apparently are good enough to take them through a reasonable variation of the story.

In kindergarten, storyboards are almost as natural to children as breathing air. After all, what child doesn't like to draw a picture and tell a story about it? The only difference is that little hands need larger paper with more drawing space. Once they have told their story, children often cut up the storyboard and make a book out of it. (I never suggest this idea, but every year, children figure it out.)

I haven't thought of all the possibilities storyboards offer, but then I don't have to. Children discover new twists for themselves. For example, despite my strong recommendation that children use pencil, one student kept drawing certain features in color. The result, for this student, was a story much richer in visual imagery. Helen, another student, found that drawing the whole story on a blackboard helped her to make changes more easily. It took me a while to see how this was different from outlining a

Figure 13   A: One day Sailor Moon and a butterfly were playing outside. B: Then the butterfly said let's have a barbeque so they did. They had hamburgers. C: All of a sudden, a monster came and he was going to eat them (Sailor Moon and the butterfly) up. D: Hah! But they threw the monster on the fire and he burned up and they all lived happily ever after.

story on a piece of paper, but it was. First, as Helen herself said, "You can see all sorts of different stories at once." She was right. It helped make her more aware of a story's endless variations. It helped me to see those possibilities and talk with her about the best way to go. I also realized that Helen's approach gave me an entirely new way to explain editing to children and teachers: instead of erasing a whole bunch of words, they could erase and change a simple drawing until they were happy with the shape of the story. Storyboards encourage individual expression, and in this way they help children find a voice.

Using Stories as Entry Points

Kieran Egan discusses the use of story as an entry to any subject in two remarkable books: *Teaching as Storytelling* (1986) and *Primary Understanding* (1988). He argues, in a fashion similar to Gardner, that any subject can be approached from the point of view of story. In fact, he claims that we should do so because of what he considers an overreliance on "logical-mathematical thinking" (1986, p. 17). He further argues that we fill children with too many facts, so that "the most powerful and energetic intellectual tools that children bring to school are largely ignored" (p. 18). One of the tools he thinks we ignore is stories. In many senses, his arguments parallel Gardner's in his attack on narrow, mechanistic kinds of curricula. (In one of those curious discoveries, I find that Egan doesn't cite Gardner and Gardner doesn't cite Egan.)

Egan outlines how stories can work as entry points in his *story form model* (1986, p. 41) and suggests entering a subject by considering what aspect of the topic would appeal to a child's feelings and thoughts. In addition, any story involves tension between at least two poles, and identifying these "binary opposites" can highlight important aspects of the subject. He cites examples as diverse as security/danger, competition/cooperation, and dependence/independence.

What Egan proposes is that teachers take these identified tensions and incorporate them into a story. This is a key point. He is asking teachers to make up a story, a dramatic event that would illustrate this binary frame. For example, it could be a moment from history, such as the Aztecs' first meeting with Cortez, or it could be the story of a village about to be flooded.

From there, the problem becomes how to seek resolution of these tensions: how the villain is defeated, the obstacle overcome, or the tension resolved is the critical point. Egan argues that children need to be involved in the problem-solving stage. Later, the teacher can initiate a review of the subject and observe what children have learned.

ENTERING KNOWLEDGE THROUGH STORIES

It was a warm spring day, but for a variety of reasons I was in a funk. At the time I was working once a week with the resource teacher, Helen Gill, and a mixed group of learners who had significant difficulty in learning to read. I had tried various techniques, none particularly remarkable, when it occurred to me that we were trying to teach skills to children who in fact had few memories and stories in which to ground those skills. They didn't have enough experience of the world to make up their own stories and thus begin to develop a sense of personal history. They took few risks and demonstrated few passions. Children like these need memorable experiences to inspire personal stories. With those stories we could enter the world of words.

I wondered how I could engage these learners. Perhaps you never really know exactly where ideas might come from, because one afternoon I was wandering around a large fruit and vegetable market near where I lived. Suddenly, my eye was drawn to ten pints of blueberries, on special because they were about to go bad. In a second, I knew the book I wanted to read (*Jamberry* by Bruce Hegen), the activity I wanted to do (making pie), and something else I wanted to try.

You know those wonderful plastic wrappings with bubbles all over them that people like to pop? I had a large roll of it from somewhere or another. After sorting out and saving the good blueberries, I still had about four quarts of fruit left.

On my way out of the store I bought some whipped cream.

The next day was bright and sunny, a fine day to be outside. We read *Jamberry* and made pies. Then I announced that there was one more thing.

By now, the children were deeply engaged in what was going on. This was fun—but it was not yet at a level of personal risk taking. We went outside. I rolled out the plastic bubble wrap and threw the blueberries out on the plastic. I took off my shoes and demonstrated how to stomp them. I added a little whipped cream, too. Now this caused some anxiety. Should they go through with it or not? Some children couldn't wait to stomp the berries, but most were cautious. This was way outside what usually happened in their lives at home or at school. Still, bit by bit, they tried it.

One student, John, sat on the stairs and absolutely refused to have anything to do with the activity. "No way," he said, in what was almost his trademark phrase. We had given up on trying to persuade him and I had gone to get the hose to start the clean up, when he jumped up off the stairs and marched through. He strutted as if he'd crossed the desert on foot.

The blueberries, the pies, the sunshine, even the old schoolyard are gone. What's left are the memories. Helen, the resource teacher, composed her own version of the story of the day in a funny little book, complete with photographs.

Some years later, I was teaching kindergarten in the school where I had stomped blueberries (well, completely rebuilt but the same location). It was fall and school had just started. There was a new girl in the class who looked a little lost, the way new students sometimes do. She sniffled and cried a little through the afternoon and kept asking how long 'til her older brother picked her up. Inevitably, the end of the day came but her older brother was late. A little annoyed, we waited.

It was John, the "no way, not me, you'll never get me into that" boy, now an adolescent. He had no idea who I was, so I said, "Blueberries. Do you remember stomping blueberries?" He gave me that blank, slightly horrified look adolescents give to adults who make no sense to them (which is most of us).

I told him to wait a minute and ran inside to get my book of photos from that day. He blinked, looked at the photos, and slowly broke into a grin. He turned to his sister. "You'll never believe what happened one day." In a real sense it had been like a rite of passage for John, the "no way, never" kid, to walk across the blueberries. It made him feel braver for having taken the risk and succeeding. It may seem that stomping blueberries is taking a risk, but consider the hesitancy of certain children to fingerpaint or get into the sandbox. Listening to him retell the story of that day, you would have sworn it was an epic adventure culminating in a great trek across a violent, crackling blue sea. Then he launched into another story of climbing up a rope ladder and another of riding his bike down a steep hill in the rain. In effect, he was going back and telling all his stories of personal risk and adventure. He was reflecting back on this moment of his life.

Through one story, he was able to enter others. That story also gave him a way to enter himself, to link memories together and play the role of older brother.

The next day his sister wanted to know if we could read the book *Jamberry* and had a lot of questions about blueberries. She had entered a new world of inquiry through John's story—and so had I.

MAKING DECISIONS

Over the years, I have begun to use Egan's model more and more. Early in the fall of one year, when I was still trying to assess where the class's interests were, I began to tell the story of a magic castle with rooms entirely of red, green, and purple. Charlene was entirely mystified. Looking around the classroom, she kept saying, "It's not green (or red or purple). Where is the red, green, and purple room?" Paulo, who was still with me, kept trying to tell her that it was in my imagination, but that just mystified her even more. "Where is it from? The nation?" she asked in a distressed tone. I stopped the story for the day.

One of the advantages of telling a story aloud is that it can be changed in any way it needs to be. It was clear that I had an engaging story but in listening to Charlene's complaint, I realized that it needed more tension. The topic, I decided, would be thinking and making decisions. I would embed the tension right in the decisions of the characters themselves and have the children think about ways of resolving the problems.

When we started the story again the next day, I would pause while the character in the story stopped and had to make decisions. Characters couldn't decide to get out of bed, which direction to go in, whether to walk or run. The characters couldn't decide anything. I announced that the class would have to be the brains of the characters in the story. As the class sat on the floor, I even made the shape of a brain around them using masking tape.

As Charlene listened, the other children became excited discussing which direction the characters should go in, how they should solve certain problems and what was behind the next door. Charlene soon got into the spirit of the discussion, and I made sure that some of her choices were honored by the characters in the story. Through this story, she caught a glimmer of the make-believe world and the world of thinking. This glimmer turned into a bright light as the months progressed. We had regular storytelling times in which one child would start a story, a second would continue it, and so on. As Charlene took her turn, her contributions became more and more imaginative, until one day she began a story for the class.

"There was a magic house but it was a make-believe house. No one could see it but Charlene—not even the teacher. In this house lived a make-believe bear. It was crying make-believe tears 'cause no one believed it except for Charlene."

Not everything that followed made sense, but what is important is that Charlene had at last entered the world of the imagination. I knew that because of her reference to make-believe. I also heard her say the word "but." In any story, there are words that suggest moments of tension, that cue a learner that something special is happening. These words can be something like "once upon a time" or "one day." For Charlene, the word was "but." It is the word that separates the world of what is from the world of what might be ("but it was a make-believe house"), the word that marks our experience off from their experience ("no one could see it but Charlene"). In other stories it can also mark time and change ("but then we moved, but then I got older"). It is the whole world of story in one word.

When I tell or read a story, I make sure that I say the word *but* with a little pause or extra emphasis so that children hear it. I select books with that specific word highlighted to give myself a chance to make that pause. I also weave the line "but one day—and there always is a one day" into a story.

By using the word "but," Charlene began to understand that stories can be used for thinking. It is a word purely of the mind. There is no such item or event in the physical world. To use it, as Charlene did, was to demonstrate an awareness of the realm of thought. It was through story that she had entered this world.

Real Versus Unreal

One day, and there always is a one day in any story, I was telling my grade three/four class of learners with exceptionalities about being careful around strangers. The context was serious. Information had been passed to the school about a person who was trying to get children into a car. I asked them to brainstorm strategies for what they might do if confronted with such a situation.

Their responses floored me. Ron suggested a whole little scenario in which "I'd turn, kick the guy, he'd scream and they'd run away." George said, "I'd take my slingshot and hit him in the eye," which struck them all as an exceptionally good idea. Now, I was pretty sure that none of them had ever seen let alone used a slingshot, so I started to get a little edgy. There is the world of make-believe and then there is the real world.

I tried to break into their little scenarios by attempting to knock down each of their solutions, but I was unsuccessful. I guessed that fear of looking straight at the scenario was a problem, but there was something else. In one of those small, inspired moments I thought of all the movies and shows I'd seen in which children *did* physically cope with dangerous adults but with cartoonish levels of violence. I realized that this was the source of all of these little stories and scripts.

As Egan would say, in this case, they were already engaged in the subject: the children had become very attached to the idea of doing harm to a stranger before he did harm to them. For binary opposites, there were large themes of security/danger, fight/flight, and underneath it all, fantasy/ reality.

It took me a moment to come up with a story that could integrate these elements into a coherent narrative. The movie *The Purple Rose of Cairo* popped into my mind. A character walks out of a movie and into the real world and finds out how difficult some movie solutions are. I told the story of a cartoon character who walked out of a cartoon and had all kinds of problems until he realized he was just a cartoon character.

I followed this up by immediately drawing a box on the chalkboard with Bart Simpson inside and another box where I drew what I called a real child. I then made the task one of telling how Bart (or any cartoon or movie character) would solve a problem and how they, as real children, would solve it. It was one of those things that worked immediately and at a deep level. The class got down to it and thought of both plausible solutions (avoid strangers, yell for help, and so on) and enacting their most car- toonish revenge on dangerous adults.

It was like finding treasure right in the classroom. The theme of real versus unreal turned up in stories again and again. We continued for a few weeks with a study of the Simpsons as a family. Among many other things, it turned out that Bart often got beat up by bullies and that he didn't always outsmart adults. "He doesn't always get away with things," cried Ronald in surprise. In fact, it seemed that he often got caught and got in trouble (which actually endeared him to the class just that much more).

This strand continued on into "trickster" folktales, in which the main character is able to fool another character through great wiles and smarts. The stories of Anansi the spider were very popular. From there we went into myths and legends of the "superheroes" of old, like Hercules and Thor. All the while, we compared what was real with what was fantastic.

The year ended before we had exhausted all the possibilities.

Before that, however, Ron suggested in a discussion that "Some stories make you feel better about not being able to do everything you want to. But you still have to be a real person, not a superhero."

We keep teaching to get to those moments.

RECOMMENDED READING

Picture Books

Myers, Walter Dean, and Ashley Bryan. *The Story of Three Kingdoms.* New York: HarperCollins, 1995.

> A folktale from Africa about stories and how they can be used to gain knowledge of the world. This story is appealing because it has a repetitive structure some children incorporate into their own storytelling. It also appeals to me because it is yet another book that talks about people thinking and learning.

Johnson, Angela, and David Soman. *Tell Me a Story, Mama.* New York: Orchard Books, 1989.

> A simple story about a mother telling stories to her daughter. It has led into discussions of who tells stories at home and to retelling some family stories, which are both poignant and hilarious. I associate this book with rainy weather because that's when kindergarten children most need to tell stories.

Luenn, Nancy, and Neil Waldman. *Nessa's Story.* New York: Macmillian, 1994.

> A story of the time when Nessa learned to tell her own story. My kindergarten classes have a strong attraction to this particular story. Many children seem to tell their own stories after they become engaged by this book.

Reference Books

Barton, Bob, and David Booth. *Stories in the Classroom: Storytelling, Reading Aloud and Roleplaying with Children.* Markham, ON: Pembroke Publishers, 1990.

A classic. This is an essential book to have if you are using stories and story-telling to enter any subject. It is full of techniques and lively accounts and examples of books and stories. This is the book that finally prodded me to learn to tell folktales.

Engel, Susan. *The Stories Children Tell: Making Sense of the Narratives of Childhood.* New York: Freeman, 1995.

There are many, many books about narrative development, but this is one of the clearest. It covers the range of research, discusses many of the factors involved when children learn to tell stories, and, above all, keeps in perspective the inherent value of storytelling to children.

14

Interlude: Thinking with Visual Media

The great divide in literacy is not between those who can read and write and those who have not yet learned to. It is between those who have discovered what kinds of literacy society values and how to demonstrate their competencies in ways that earn recognition.

MARGARET MEEK

On Being Literate

We all remember the story of Helen Keller. Rendered blind, deaf, and mute by illness as a young child, she existed for many years without really understanding language until one day, through the patient efforts of her teacher, Annie Sullivan, she realized that everything had a name. From that point on there was no stopping her as she discovered language. I have never witnessed anything that dramatic, but I have come close.

Omar is one of the most remarkable learners I have ever met. When he first came to school he barely spoke or even played. His kindergarten teacher, Sharon McMahon, had noticed odd little strengths; for example, he could read the name cards of children in the class. He was also continually watching the world as if trying to make a connection between himself and what was going on around him.

I first met him when he was six and had entered a segregated class for learners with significant language difficulties. Sharon went along with him as the teacher of the class, while I was the consulting speech-language pathologist. Ordinarily, I do not find much value in such segregated classes, but Sharon ran this class on the absolute belief that following children's play initiatives would build all forms of cognition.

The class was better than any soap opera. There was always some new script or play going on—weddings, trips to the beach, meals at restaurants of all kinds. Most of the time, our role was to respond to what was going on, although it was not always easy. For example, we wondered where to draw the line when a long wedding scenario, which took weeks to play out, drifted toward the inevitable honeymoon. Fortunately, the play shifted direction to scenarios of eating in fast-food restaurants.

After an initial period of adjustment (he screamed regularly for six weeks), Omar began to discover language. He started to talk in ways that made sense to others and, finding himself understood, began to talk non-stop. He even began to remember times when he did not talk. As his language developed, his tremendous visual concentration also continued to develop. He loved computers and would happily engage in any activity on the computer. His sight word vocabulary, almost the first aspect of language that had developed, continued to expand, and he began reading pattern books. In so many ways, any language for Omar was like a second language. His first was rooted in a visual, spatial world I realized I couldn't imagine.

One day I arrived to observe an interesting piece of domestic play. A couple of the children, including Omar, slowly constructed a television set out of an old box. They "watched" it for a few minutes but then announced that "nothing was on." I thought, well that's the end of that—but, as is often the case, I thought too soon.

Omar and Dwayne began to collect materials to build a video game attachment to the television. Eventually they made objects that did resemble joysticks and a player. They added a few sound effects and some occasional commentary, but there was very little talking other than to argue about whose turn it was and what game they were going to play next. The games seemed to change quickly and from what little conversation there was, I couldn't follow what was happening. When I asked Omar if he could "see" what was happening, he paused a moment. Then, without taking his eyes off the "television," he said, "Yes. Can't you?"

———

THE NATIVE TONGUE OF THE ELECTRONIC MEDIA

The electronic media are often regarded as the enemy of thinking. This story of Omar playing the imaginary video game, barely moving and barely talking, would seem to be an example of the effect of an imagination-killing technology at work. Furthermore, many teachers would agree with Gavriel Salomon, for example, who notes that certain forms of media presentation, such as music videos, may encourage "a preference for a quick paced, erratic, even chaotic way of handling information" (1997, p. 379).

I remain skeptical of such claims. I have met many children who lived in chaotic conditions and, yes, they had incredibly short attention spans, but this could hardly be laid at the feet of the electronic media. I suspect that children develop chaotic ways of handling information when the adults around them are in chaos. Indeed, Salomon notes that the presence of adult mediation makes a difference in how effectively children use and respond to the media.

Moreover, I have encountered too many examples of children with learning difficulties who still seemed to have a natural facility for working with video equipment or computers. I have watched films with poor readers who nonetheless made accurate predictions about what would happen next based on a change in the lighting.

This sort of skill is hardly confined to children with special needs. Paulo almost certainly thinks in images some of the time and has made up his own live-action video games involving the whole class, complete with characters and special powers. One day Michael announced that he knew how to read maps because he "saw them in the video game" he had played.

Indeed, there may be more of these kinds of visual-spatial skills around than there used to be. Salomon (1997) reports on a number of studies indicating that the more children were exposed to television and film in thoughtful ways, the more comfortable they became in understanding the unique visual and spatial codes and conventions of the media. I wonder if the various electronic media (television, video, computers, the Internet) actually help children like Omar. Such children seem to have some natural affinity for the visual nature of the media. As Gardner has said, "Quite possibly those whose 'native tongue' is television will eventually become its greatest poets" (Gardner and Jaglom 1982, p. 251).

It is not hard to see this "native tongue" at work if you watch and listen carefully. It turns up in play, in storytelling, in the very way children think. Omar may have been on to something when he suggested that it was *I* who could not see. For all I know, he really was imagining pieces of a game but could not explain it to me. As evidence for this, I turn back to Paulo, who has no difficulty explaining his thoughts to me.

Paulo joined up with Michael, Blaine, and Nicolas to create their own living video game. They did not use the latest technology but it inspired them to create play scenarios in which they took on the roles of superheroes they had invented, each with different superpowers. This was not mere play, for there was an enormous amount of stopping to discuss the rules. They also used very stylized movements, which they discussed for plausibility and "aesthetic" value ("that's a very cool move").

Throughout their play, which lasted for weeks, I occasionally inquired how they knew something was a "cool" move or how they had decided on a sequence of rules. They usually referred to some video game or a character on a television show where there was a similar rule. About one spinning move Paulo said, "It's like he has to spin before he throws a cold bomb or else the cold isn't as cold as it should be." When I mentioned that this move reminded me of dance videos we had been watching, Paulo slapped his head and announced, "There could be a new hero who wears the tap shoes except when he taps, it makes like lightning bolts come out." As he said this, I could see that the entire group was picturing this possibility.

The "native tongue" of the electronic media is not confined to play. It also shows up in children's daily storytelling. I take this idea from a local storyteller, Dan Yashinsky, who observed that his son appeared to be telling a story the way television did. There were moments when he seemed to be framing a shot. Since that time, I have often heard children include this kind of visual "framing" in their narratives. Alex, for example, often told a story that had bits like "and then the rabbit looked like . . . surprise! [Alex made a surprised face, his hands framing his face] and the alien looked like he was seeing a ghost [here Alex made a scared face, his hands again framing his face]." When I think back on it, I realize that Omar used to tell stories just like this, only he used more gestures and fewer words. The influences of our visual culture penetrate both play and storytelling. It is worth noting, however, that the play of Paulo and his friends and Alex's stories use the language of the visual world to create new meanings.

SOME IMPLICATIONS OF COMPUTERS FOR LITERACY AND THINKING

As early as 1983, Gardner, writing with Salomon, commented that using computers would "include the mastery of ordinary (natural) language as well as whatever literate linguistic and mathematical abilities appear to 'constitute' or to be required by programming language" (p. 31). They also noted that computers would involve a variety of symbolic forms, such as music, charts, and maps. At that time, computers involved "considerable linguistic and logical mathematical intelligence" but Gardner and Salomon wondered if advances in technology would ultimately make the computer a tool offering many possibilities for the greatest range of symbol systems (p. 31). They anticipated the rise of multimedia applications in which musicians, artists, storytellers, and publishers use computers to create new kinds of reference books, stories, and games.

At the heart of all of this is the "relational database," which is a database that connects data by some form of association. It is possible to link word and picture, picture and sound, word and sound. This is the engine that has driven the explosion in multimedia products, in which sound, animation, pictures, words, icons, and so on are linked together.

Relational databases also form the basis of some of the Internet. Anyone who has "surfed" the Internet will know how easy it is to go from one subject to the next simply by following divergent threads. For example, I can start by looking for information about multiple intelligences, move onto other theories of intelligence, go to a particular thinking skills program at a particular school, and end up browsing through course catalogues at a particular university.

Many teachers, however, may have little or no access to computers and teach students like mine who rarely have computers at home. I have wondered over the years if there aren't ways of teaching children the "native tongue" of computers without computers themselves. Again, the answer may be much closer than many teachers realize. When we use semantic webbing, brainstorming, or any of a number of visual organizers, we are probably using tools that are a direct offshoot of working with computers

(Hyerle 1996). Such tools help to organize information, but they may also teach children about an underlying structure they'll need in the information age.

Relational databases also show up in narrative forms. When I first read a "pick-your-own-stories" book, I was struck by its format—at various points, the reader makes a choice on behalf of a character. If the reader decides to, say, fight the dragon, then he turns to a certain page. If he makes a different choice, he goes to an entirely different page. There is obviously more than one possible ending to the story. If diagrammed, it would naturally end up forming a web. Such books come in many forms. Some contain mostly picture puzzles with few words. Others are adventure-type stories with storylines and settings that range from the Old West and outer space to the here and now. There are also books that use the format to teach history and geography (Packer 1988) or replay a sports game (Strupp 1994).

"Pick-your-own-stories" books include both narrative and logical-sequential forms. Choices are framed in *if/then* statements, *either/or* statements, and *but* statements: *If* you do this, *then* that will happen. You may choose *either* this *or* that. This can happen *but* not this.

I wonder if, in reading these books, learners aren't being prepared for the "native tongue" of computer programming and if, in writing such books, children actually get a taste of the planning and logic such a story (and, by implication, a computer program) requires.

Recently, Karen Devonish, a French teacher, and her grade four class did one in French as part of a teacher research project on how to improve her class's written language. She set a simple context, an adventure in their neighborhood. The class listed places they might go and planned ahead to link them with others. Students then chose an individual location, described what they might find there, and set up a choice within the story. Then—and this is not so easy—they had to make sure that the whole story worked, which means all the multiple choices and multiple endings.

When I read such student writing, I return to Margaret Meek's words at the beginning of this chapter. The essence of a multiple intelligence classroom is, I think, to create opportunities for all children to discover the kinds of literacies society values and find a way to express themselves. These new technologies are more likely to afford children as diverse as Omar and Paulo these opportunities and to create new ways for all students to be successful thinkers and to see themselves as thinkers.

Figure 14   A sample from the story, helpfully translated from the French by the students in Ms. Devonish's class.

You go to a pool and decide to take a swim. You jump from the diving board into the pool. If you see a turtle, go to page 11. If you do not see a turtle, go to page 14 <div align="right">*Rachel*</div>	You see a turtle in the pool. You think you might want to take it. If you decide to take the turtle, turn to page 12. If you do not want to take it, turn to page 19. <div align="right">*Emmanuelle*</div>
You want to keep the turtle. It is very small. You love and take care of the turtle forever. The end. <div align="right">*Toraj*</div>	After having seen the turtle, you leave the pool and go to Wendy's. You eat a hamburger and drink some juice. When you finish eating you go home for a nap. THE END <div align="right">*Cortney*</div>

WRITE A "PICK-YOUR-OWN-ENDING" STORY

You and your class can create a "pick-your-own-ending" story with a set of filing cards, some yarn, and your collective imagination. (If you are one of those with computers powerful enough to program multimedia, go directly to the Recommended Reading list!)

Warning! Keep it simple to start!

Imagine a setting—a castle, a planet, a house, for example. (I strongly suggest making it a condition that there be no serious bloodshed in this world.)

Define the parameters of this world:

- How many rooms/places can you go? (to start, one per each member of a class or one per group)

- How many main characters? (limit the number to one or two)

- How many ways in and out of a room/place should there be? (keep it simple)

Decide, in advance, what rooms/places link together (this relates to the number of choices possible in each).

Decide how many endings the story will have (three or four is best for a first try).

Give each student a file card. On one side, ask the student to sketch out what their room or area looks like. On the other side, ask them to write

- a couple of simple sentences to describe the room

- the choices in that room (one or two, including how to get in or out)

- a concluding sentence in an if/then form that confirms what the consequence of the choice is (If you want to go out the green door, then go to the yellow room; if you want to go out the red door, then go to the purple room.) Those students responsible for one of the endings should make sure their card offers no further choices and the story concludes.

Make an overall flowchart. As the file cards are completed in rough form, put them together on a wall. You will want to be sure that the story pieces fit together and that all choices lead to one of the endings.

All sorts of complications can be introduced, such as magical powers that don't work in one part of this world ("But the wand doesn't work in the green room.") or special rooms/places at the very center that connect to all other rooms.

Keep it simple to start! Remember, students are writing more than a story; they are writing a simple computer program!

Note: As I was writing this book, I discovered another format, which I would also recommend (see Smith 1996).

RECOMMENDED READING

Pick-Your-Own-Ending Stories

Burston, P., and A. Graham. *The Funfair of Evil.* London: Walker Books, 1990.

Montgomery, R. A. *The Haunted House.* Toronto: Bantam Books, 1981.

Packard, Edward. *America: Why Is There an Eye on the Pyramid on the One Dollar Bill?* Toronto: McGraw Hill, 1988.

Strupp, Peter. *You Call the Play, Baseball: Catcher in Command.* Toronto: Bantam Books, 1994.

Reference Books

Meek, Margaret. *On Being Literate.* London: Bodley Head Children's Books, 1991.

Margaret Meek has written many excellent books and articles on literacy. This book in particular is a readable set of meditations about the nature of literacy and how it has changed and may change over time.

Turkle, Sherry. *Life on the Screen: Identity in the Age of the Internet.* New York: Simon and Schuster, 1995.

More marvelous questions and meditations about computers and identity. Turkle is interested in how new technologies change us and afford us the opportunities to exercise aspects of ourselves that we may not have been aware of before. While she spends more time talking about adults, the book is relevant to teachers interested in what future literacies may look like.

15

Thinking Counts: Logical/Quantitative Reasoning

A mathematician, like a painter or a poet, is a maker of patterns.

G. B. HARDY

A Mathematician's Apology

From their writing I realized that my grade five/six class could use some mini-lessons on prefixes and suffixes to help with spelling. In addition, a number of them were learning English as a second language and needed to work on comprehension as well as spelling.

I hit upon the idea of introducing "number" prefixes. For example, "bi," in *bicycle,* means two of something. I considered the lesson from a variety of perspectives and thought it could work on a number of levels for a number of the children. It was short and would allow me to demonstrate an approach to the topic. I began by pointing out that math was everywhere, even in words. In general, the class seemed to catch on to the basic idea of "number" prefixes after a little discussion, and I asked for a few more examples before sending them on to the next task. Bit by bit, the examples came: bilingual, triceratops. Then Kevin, an inspired gleam in his eye, shouted "Bi! Bisexual!" He began to define it, but before I could tell him not to bother, he said, "Tri! Trisexual!" The class was off to the races attaching number prefixes to every vaguely sexual word they knew.

Pandemonium broke out, of course, and I was left scrambling to redirect the discussion. The opportunity presented itself when someone asked what "trisexual" meant. A few made guesses. After a moment, someone put forward the suggestion that it might have something to do with a "ménage à trois." Seizing the moment, I agreed that you never know, it just might, and suggested they ask the French teacher that very afternoon. Then I quickly changed the subject.

Fortunately, the French teacher has a very good sense of humor.

Despite this rocky start, the logical-quantitative entry point has proven to be one of the easiest to use because it offers so many possibilities. Each aspect of logical-quantitative thinking—number, measurement, classification, definition, logic, procedure, and so on—could rate a separate discussion. Taken together, they constitute a whole way of representing, filtering, and creating information about the world. Some children and adults use this kind of thinking all the time, in every aspect of their lives, and all of us use it some of the time: we count, we measure, we rate. Indeed, counting, measuring, and sequencing are so intrinsic to our nature that they overlap with all the other intelligences. For example, we analyze the body's performance by measuring speed and distance. Music and mathematics are so closely intertwined that many writers have commented on the relationship (Hofstadter 1979; Gardner 1983).

Even the act of reading offers examples of quantitative thinking. In teaching children to read, for example, we often count words and letters in order to develop a sense that words, sounds, and letters are individual units of language (Wallach and Miller 1988). Children learn to speak of "long" words and "short" stories, and many consider it a personal breakthrough when they begin to read books with numbered pages. In discussing books, we begin to refer to pages such and such.

In a world where everything can be enumerated, young children soon become regular counters (Gardner 1991, p. 88). Four-year-olds, according to Gardner, begin to turn a "digital" lens on the world, counting everything that can be counted. They also come to have theories about how numbers should operate. Given these conditions, Gardner again wonders what goes wrong in schools if adults have difficulty in solving relatively simple algebraic equations, and older children in learning fractions and numbers. Even those who create computer programs can make incorrect assumptions.

He characterizes the problem as one of "rigidly applied algorithms" (p. 159). Math is taught in schools through procedures and formulas. But schools do not take children inside these procedures and formulas to understand how they work. He shows how often we are deceived by our natural language systems: we take things for granted, we assume too much, and we don't reason mathematically. We settle for the "correct answer compromise": educators think they have done something if learners can at least plug numbers into a formula.

But if we want children to reason mathematically, we have to teach them to understand the structures they are applying rather than just how to fill in a number set. Gardner points out children's intuitive understanding of math: they have some concept of money, for example, and thus a basis for the decimal system; they know about pizza, which can introduce fractions.

I would be the first to admit, however, that it is easy enough to say these things but not always as easy to do them. I've struggled, and continue to struggle, with "correct answer compromise" teaching in mathematics. Knowing how much structure to provide and when is always an open question.

BEYOND THE CORRECT ANSWER COMPROMISE: MATH TALK

The English language includes many words that represent mathematical concepts: *adding, taking away, multiplying* and *dividing* are part of children's "intuitive" understanding of mathematical ideas. I have already pointed out that number prefixes are embedded in English words, but I also want to mention everyday words like *corner,* a more visual equivalent of math words like *vertices.*

Here, I would suggest, lies a possible solution to the "correct answer compromise." A few years ago I attended a great workshop given by Tom Brissenden. He described what he called "math talk," demonstrating ways in which an ambiguous question like "How many lines are in a corner?" could nudge learners to discover and define their terms. He outlines this approach in detail in *Talking About Mathematics* (1988), one of many books now available on the subject (see also Pimm 1987; Beesey and Davie 1994).

Brissenden, too, has a framework, which he refers to as "do, talk, and record." First, children have an experience of some kind involving mathematics—measuring an area with some cubes, for example, or counting the number of people at a table. Then they pair that experience with talk: the teacher poses additional challenges and children discuss and reflect on their own understandings. Finally, children try to make some record of their findings through pictures, diagrams, words, or numbers.

"Math talk" gave me a number of ideas for going beyond the "correct answer compromise." I played with some of them from time to time but it was only when a group of teachers came to our center to do teacher research that the idea of "math talk" every day really grabbed my attention.

Now, I have never been especially comfortable with show-and-tell, which is odd, considering that it is an oral language activity and I do so much teaching through talk. I suppose it strikes me as too much a one-size-fits-all vehicle; some children are good at it and could talk forever, while others have to be painfully drawn out. I have often wondered if it is the children who least need the practice who get the most air time. Still, children in kindergarten expect show-and-tell and are constantly trying to introduce it into my classroom. (It doesn't matter if they haven't been to school anywhere else. It seems to be part of children's general assumptions about school.)

So, I set up a time of the day for math talk. A learner brings in an object and analyzes it from the perspectives of size, shape, color, and number. The object is mundane and common—the clothes the child is wearing, a doll, a piece of Lego, and so on. I'll often ask questions like:

"What numbers do you see in this?"

"What patterns are in this—what happens over and over again?"

"How many colors are on it?"

"How many lines can you see? What kinds of lines are they—fat, straight, curved?"

The children come to know these questions so well they can rattle them off.

Listen to Joseph, discussing his shirt:

"It's got um . . . [counts] seven colors. There is some fat lines here [points] and . . . some wiggly lines here [points]. I see some circles."

"How many?" I ask.

Joseph counts. "Six on this side [meaning one sleeve] and six on the other—that's uh, um twelve! And this is the biggest shirt for me—all my others are small from when I was little."

I help, as in this example, by encouraging the child to count or look at a specific part, or by asking prompting questions. I also introduce other objects for comparison of overall size, weight, length, and/or height. Later in the year we put objects in the water table and notice that some big objects float while some small ones sink. For smaller objects, we use the balance scale to make comparisons.

Once children get into the habit of describing an object using number, I introduce "procedural" talk. Here, children talk about how something works and what steps to take to make it work. Again, our emphasis is on the ordinary: zippers on coats, shoelaces on shoes, Velcro, wheels on toy cars—all are examples we have investigated. In a more difficult variation, I'll ask children to speculate on *how* something is made. How does the toy get in the package? How do they make soda pop fizzy? It is interesting to hear their answers, because, of course, I have no idea how any of this is done either. At the same time, learning to guess and hypothesize is also a form of math talk (Brissenden 1988).

Such simple talk can lead to small investigations, such as how many Lego pieces it takes to cross the carpet (eighty-five). We read a book on how the fizz gets into soda pop. We have also classified books by color one day, by author another, by size on still another. Some children obviously do better than others, but all are using their logical-mathematical intelligence to enter and investigate the world. Their knowledge counts.

Using Math Talk as an Entry Point

Procedures   The best questions are the ones for which you genuinely want an answer. The kindergarten children and I had been talking about how things work, especially some moving toys that all have to be wound up or operated in some way. Once or twice, I had also wondered how something was made, but I hadn't really pursued an answer.

One day, however, I was holding a doll that Melanie had brought in for math talk. It had long, fine hair. I wondered how the manufacturer got the hair on the head and what it was made of. Hands shot up.

"First they make the hair, then they glue it on," said Paulo.

"No, first they make the head, then they glue on [the hair]," countered Faiza.

"The glue is on the inside," said Cherelle. "You can't see it on the outside."

Several other comments continued in this vein. Nicolas, meanwhile, was madly waving his hand. "I know how they make it. First, they get plastic and put it in a machine and make it thin. Then another machine pushes it through the doll's head and they stick it by melting it."

That ended the discussion. I have no idea if this is accurate and Nicolas's parents don't work in factories that make dolls, but none of us could think of anything to add to his description.

I asked Nicolas to make me a picture of the process, but he declined. "I don't know how to draw it, just talk about it."

Some learners are organized right from the day you meet them. Ask them to search for a coat and they methodically retrace their steps. They love counting books early on and have neat and tidy desks. To me, these are the children with a deeper affinity for the computer. They not only like going there they are the first to learn to load programs, fix software glitches, and, as I have occasionally discovered to my surprise, reprogram certain parts of the computer.

We often overlook this intelligence in its different forms. I have observed learners with clear language difficulties who still experienced success in procedural knowledge. Jonathon, for example, understood schedules and routines long before he mastered talking about time.

Step-by-step procedures structure every aspect of our daily lives, and for many learners, they are the best place to start teaching. After all, many of them are nothing if not practical. Getting a drink from a vending machine, walking to the corner store, and operating a VCR incorporate many skills and symbol systems in real-world ways. For learners with a limited capacity, they should be the first instructional strategy. After all, if you start with a practical skill, you never need to worry about how to transfer it from the classroom to the real world.

Helen Gill, a resource teacher, invented what she called her "talk tokens." Essentially, she took an activity that had a sequence, such as a science experiment, and illustrated it with drawings on four cards. The first card always had a green sticker, meaning first and "go." The last card always had a red sticker, meaning "stop." Using this model, she was able to create situations that helped children understand procedure, pivot words, and finally, expository and explanatory kinds of talk.

Using these cards, children would do all sorts of experiments and talk them through: first we did this *and then* we did this *and then* we did this and then it was over. It was procedural, logical, expository talk. Once

Figure 15a-d   Helen's cards record simple science and cooking instructions that anyone can follow.

children were able to use and understand this basic language, they could respond to challenges (make your own record of an activity or tell us about a sequence without the cards).

Eventually, the question of how to teach the idea underlying *because* interested us. We tried different approaches but couldn't seem to demonstrate it clearly. Then, one day, in one of those curious moments of learning, I found myself talking to Raymond and trying, with little success it seemed, to explain the meaning of the word. Raymond used the word, but only to start a sentence, not to connect two ideas together. However, at one point in the discussion, Raymond said, "Oh, you mean go *this* way," and made a backwards gesture with his hand (he was a learner with great bodily-kinesthetic awareness). I hadn't meant to indicate going backwards but had inadvertently swept my hands backwards to indicate "start over again." This gesture unlocked the moment for both of us.

What I learned was that in illustrating a sequence, start with the last event in the sequence and work back toward the beginning. This is how you could illustrate causality. You could say the soup was made *because* we put it on the stove to cook, we chopped up the vegetables, and we added the spices and the water. Words are not always that simple to illustrate but this was one way to give learners a handle on it.

Teaching Classification   Classification is a tool we use in every area of life. We organize and classify people, objects, and places. We classify plants and animals. We classify by aesthetic features, by quantity, and by impressions. We represent classification through webbing, Venn diagrams, and charts. This aspect of the logical-quantitative entry point has innumerable applications.

One common math talk challenge was "Does it go with things you like, things you wear, things you eat, or things you share?," a simple little rhyme I dreamed up to get the children to begin thinking in categories. Occasionally, someone would want to put an item into two different categories. Alex once brought in a cheese string and wore it around his wrist to show that he could do other things with it besides eat it. The idea that an object could fit in more than one category was a little bewildering to the children at first, but most began to understand the idea after a while. On one recent occasion, the children demonstrated the extent to which they understood.

Every time I read a book to the children, I begin by mentioning the author and the illustrator. This is only fair to authors and illustrators, but it also teaches children that someone made this story and that they can make stories too. It also shows children that they can group books according to author.

This is the kind of classification librarians do—but so, apparently, do kindergarten children on snowy days. I must have been looking outside at the snow because I didn't quite notice that all the books in the book corner had been taken off the shelves and were now sitting in large piles. When I did finally notice, I assumed that the children had been directed to do so by another adult. I couldn't conceive of any other reason.

The level of discussion among the three boys who made the piles, however, was far too intense and committed to be simply a response to adult direction. As it turned out, they had thought up the idea of making some of their favorite books and authors easier to find, "like in the library." So, Dr. Seuss books were being separated from the piles, as were Robert Munsch books. Here and there lay a few scattered favorites in a separate pile. The rest were in large piles. The boys were creating their own personal catalogue.

But there was a problem.

"I can't decide if this one goes in the pile I like or in the pile that's for Dr. Seuss books," said Nicolas.

"It's a Dr. Seuss book. It goes with a Dr. Seuss pile," said Kevin.

"That's true," said Paulo, "but we already put a Robert Munsch book in the good books and the rest in two places, the 'good' pile and the Robert Munsch pile."

"Aha! So I *can* put it two places!" cried a triumphant Nicolas. A moment later he said, "But I don't have two books." It was a problem not easily solved, but at least they had come to understand categorization.

Defining   Defining is another critical component of logical and mathematical thinking. Any subject involves defining conditions, from history ("this era runs from 1929 to 1941") to science ("this animal is defined by its red markings"). Even at the highest levels of mathematics, it is often essential to define the parameters according to which a problem-solving activity is taking place. This way of thinking is so widely applicable children should get used to it early.

To *define* means to frame the members of a set so exactly and exclusively, one knows what would be a member of the set and what wouldn't. The more specific, precise, and rule-driven one can be, the better. This kind of skill isn't rare, it is only rarely articulated.

A vintage pattern book has helped me in teaching children the basics of defining. Margaret Wise Brown's *The Important Book* (1949) contains wonderful patterns for beginning definers, for example, "Apples are red, apples are round . . . but the important thing about an apple is that it is white inside." Books like this give a model for formulating definitions. I have employed *The Important Book* and seen others use it throughout the grades. With older children, the writing and vocabulary can become more and more precise. However, with kindergarten children, I have found it easiest to integrate into our daily math talk. I read the book aloud and invite the children to come up with their own "important" definitions.

Children who are challenged to use this pattern are able to tackle other problems, like defining shapes ("The important thing about a square is that there are four sides and they are all the same," said Paulo) or corners ("It's where three lines come into each other—like crashing!" said Alex). This is the beginning of a deeper understanding of mathematics. More broadly, however, children who understand this aspect of a logical-quantitative thinking can approach any topic or field of study and uncover its rules, assumptions, and parameters. For example, Kedemah said, "The important thing about a sweater is that you wear it. It is red and green and it's big but you wear it." Jerome said of his truck, that it has "lots of colors. It has four wheels. The important thing is that you play with it." Jordana defined her stuffed animal, "It's soft. It's my friend. It's a bear. But the important thing is you can hug it." On learning about light bulbs, Funsho said, "The important thing about them is that they need electricity. They make light and heat but they have to have electricity."

Children identify, list, and define the common characteristics of many things but the important thing is that they are starting to think about *how* to do it.

Number   We live in a world of numbers. A simple walk through the school on any given day finds catalogues with prices, telephone numbers, books classified according to the Dewey decimal system, books with page numbers, books about numbers, scales, rulers, games, and on and on. I have sent children on "number hunts" to try to find all the kinds of numbers they can. Number is probably the one aspect of the logical-quantitative entry point teachers already use. We conduct surveys to make graphs, we look at countries through population, geography through distance, history through dates, school through grades, assessment through scores, and this doesn't begin to consider the study of number in and of itself and as it applies to measurement.

We are surrounded by number, yet solving problems involving number can be difficult. Much of this is probably related to our emphasis on number as a collection of facts like times tables rather than as a tool to use and discover with. This returns us to Gardner's notion of "correct answer compromise."

Creating opportunities for even young children to explore the idea of number encourages them to perceive patterns, find relationships, and use numbers to enumerate everything, including themselves. In my kindergarten class, the book *Each Orange Had 8 Slices: A Counting Book* (Giganti 1992) was a huge success. It features text like this: "On my way to school I saw three little kids. Each kid rode a tricycle. Each tricycle had three wheels." The book goes on to ask about how many children there were, how many trikes, and how many wheels altogether.

I had assumed that the intricacies of the pattern and the questions would interest only a few. I was wrong. The book was wildly popular, and we ended up adding a second copy to the classroom bookshelves. The questions were engaging and children got practice in actually counting up the answers.

Still, I was surprised when Micheal stood up in front of the group one day for math talk and said, "On my way to school I saw a boy with two hands. Each hand had five fingers. How many fingers were there?"

The class sat quietly for a moment. Then, instead of answering his question, they all tried to come up with their own. With some prompting, they proposed questions like these:

"On my way to school I saw two girls. Each girl had a head. How many heads were there?"

"On my way to school, I saw three toy cars. Each toy car had four wheels. How many cars are there? How many wheels are there?"

"On my way to school, I saw three boys. Each boy had two feet. Each foot had one shoe. How many boys were there? How many shoes? How many feet?"

This number pattern has proven very effective for understanding many applicable number in the world. It's worth investigating.

Measurement   Another vast area for logical-quantitative reasoning is measurement. We measure time, distance, size, and weight. We compare interesting trivia, the height of a famous building, the length of a vehicle, the weight of an animal, the length of time since someone lived, and so on. Consider the case of dinosaurs. Children are fascinated by their size, the size of their teeth, the speed at which they could move, the amount of food they ate, and the length of time since they became extinct. It is possible to study dinosaurs from the perspective of measurement alone.

However, measurement in general is also full of odd and intriguing challenges. Wondering how many Lego pieces it takes to cover a carpet, how many bottles of water it takes to fill up a fish tank, at what angle to build a ramp so a toy car can fly over a wall can send children to investigate. Exploring different "units" for measuring an area (string, meter sticks, human feet, bodies) or a container (glasses of water, rocks, pebbles, dice, toy cars) has kept many children engaged for long stretches of time.

The point of all of this measuring? To get children to understand the problems of measurement, such as comparison (Which one is bigger?), variables (Can two people make a puzzle faster than one person?) and different measuring devices. Around the time of one of the Olympics, students watched a lot of sports on television and began talking about world records for being fastest at putting on a coat or holding their breath. We actually tried watching the wall clock to see how many seconds had passed while holding our breath, but it was difficult to see. Then I introduced a stopwatch to the class. The first thing we found out was that it only took thirty seconds to learn to use it. We also declared our own "world records." It took three minutes and twenty seconds for Amy and Beslayne to completely paint my hand over with magic marker. It took Micheal six and three-tenths seconds to say the entire alphabet. The children could tidy up in four minutes and eleven seconds, a fact I found very interesting. But there is nothing like an argument to promote deeper learning.

Ours was over a "world record" for doing a puzzle (13.4 seconds). The previous world record holder, Bernice, complained, "That's not fair. The puzzle only had twenty pieces. And it was an easy puzzle. And they had two people making the puzzle. My puzzle had thirty pieces. How long would it take one of them to make my puzzle?"

There was some grumbling, but it was generally accepted that Bernice had a point. So the question became one of finding another puzzle with an equal number of pieces and making sure that only one person worked on it at a time. Once this was done, Bernice again held the record for a day. Not satisfied, however, Shane commented that one thirty-piece puzzle was made of large pieces while the other had small pieces. The children measured with their rulers and indeed, one puzzle was bigger than another. At one point, Paulo tried to count the little twists and turns of some of the pieces to see "if there are more sides on bigger pieces," but the task proved too much even for his extraordinary powers of concentration. (For the record, though, he lay on the floor practically motionless for twenty-one minutes and eleven seconds trying to figure it out.)

In the end, the interest in the problem fizzled out when the class discovered that Bernice could make *any* puzzle faster than anybody. In the process, they had considered variables of measurement, time, and quantity. Their learning was quantifiable.

Math Talk in Action: Cooking   There are so many aspects to the logical-quantitative entry point, it is hard to focus on just one. I try to find activities or topics that naturally integrate several aspects of mathematical reasoning at once. For example, studying the toys in any era or from any part of the world involves number, definition, classification, procedure, and measurement, as does any study of people in any era or from any part of the world. But there is a more satisfying way: cooking. Cooking is one of the most integrated mathematical activities I know. There are step-by-step *sequences* to follow. There are *numbers* of vegetables to be cut, *amounts* of rice to be made, *cups* of water to be *added,* and *numbers* of place settings to be arranged. *Time* becomes important at different stages: measuring *how long* it takes to do certain activities and how long to leave something in the oven. We *classify* food waste as good or not so good for the worms in our composter. We distinguish fruits from vegetables, fish from chicken, dessert from the main meal. We *schedule* turns at cooking. We look back over time at what we have made in the past in our *monthly* recipe books.

On Thursday mornings at our center, enticing aromas waft from the childcare area. It is Thursday hot lunch with a guest chef, a new recipe, and three or four children, who are doing almost all the chopping, peeling, stirring, and pouring. When lunch is served, the recipe is critiqued by the earnest palates of three-, four-, and five-year-olds.

Listen as Blaine, Jordana, and Richmond prepare a meal.

"How much carrots do we chop?" asks Blaine.

"That's a biggest carrot I ever chop," says Richmond.

"Is that small enough?" inquires Jordana about the carrot she has chopped.

"What's next? The potatoes?" asks Blaine.

"The oven says six. Does that mean it's hot?" says Jordana.

"How many times do I stir [the pot]?" asks Richmond.

"Five people sit at this table so I need five cups, five spoons, and five bowls," calculates Jordana.

"Is this a stirring spoon or a other kind [ladle]?" asks Richmond.

"The worms eat the tops of the carrots," says Blaine as he sorts them from the carrots.

"It is finished. Time to eat," Jordana announces.

Cooking is about more than just math talk. It is about other people and places.

We try to invite guest chefs to cook dishes from their particular culture. It is also about personal responsibility and safety: children handle knives, stir hot pots, and wash their hands before handling food. It is about science: boiling points, nutrition, and classifying leftovers we can feed the worms. It is about literacy. The childcare wrote their own cookbook, *Why Cook with Kids?* and the children not only tested and sampled the recipes, they helped to write the book. The center puts out a monthly newsletter with pictures of the previous month's cooks and their recipes.

Above all else, cooking is about a sense of accomplishment. You feed yourself, you feed others, and you do it with your own hands. What more can you ask from an activity?

Figure 15e   Nicolas chopping parsley for cooking. Notice that he has arranged the sprigs of parsley in order of size.

RECOMMENDED READING

Picture Books

Atherly, Sara, and Megan Halsey. *Math in the Bath (and Other Fun Places, Too!)* New York: Simon and Schuster Books for Young Readers, 1995.

> Math everywhere! This is a marvelous book for demonstrating many different places and topics (such as nature, the dinner table). It will generate ideas for math talk.

Brown, Margaret Wise. *The Important Book.* Illus. L. Weisgard. New York: Harper and Row, 1949.

> Yes, the examples are a little dated and there is always some discussion about what's important (''*I* think the most important thing about an apple is that you eat it'') but it is still a useful model after all of these years.

Giganti, Paul. *Each Orange Had 8 Slices: A Counting Book*. Illus. Donald Crews. New York: Greenwillow Books, 1992.

Patterns, counting, classification, and simple algebraic formulations in a colorfully illustrated picture book. It is always a popular title among kindergarten children.

Schwartz, David M., and Steven Kellogg. *How Much Is a Million?* New York: William Morrow, 1985.

This book illustrates both bigger and bigger numbers and the places that would be needed to hold such great amounts.

Scieszka, Jon, and Lane Smith. *Math Curse*. New York: Penguin Books, 1995.

Probably the funniest math book ever written. It is also an outstanding survey of math in all aspects of life. Even young children get some of the humor, but I have also seen some marvelous new versions written by older children.

Reference Books

Baker, Dave, Cheryl Semple, and Tony Stead. *How Big Is the Moon?: Whole Maths in Action*. Portsmouth, NH: Heinemann, 1990.

This is one of my favorite math books because it captures the spirit of investigation through mathematics. It is also adopts the principles of whole language in teaching mathematics.

Brissenden, Tom. *Talking About Mathematics: Mathematical Discussions in Primary Classrooms*. Oxford: Basil Blackwell, 1988.

It may be hard to get this book, but it is a great resource for anyone who wants to go beyond the basics and delve into mathematics. Brissenden gives many examples of how he would set up a sound program for mathematical understanding, including (of course) possible schedules. The book has many samples of children's talk and written work.

Lake, Joanne. *Imagine: A Literature-Based Approach to Science*. Markham, ON: Pembroke Publishers, 1993.

If you like the idea of using children's literature to enter math and science, you'll love this book. The author has compiled a very usable list of all types of childrens literature.

Veitch, Beverly, and Thelma Harms. *Cook and Learn: A Child's Cookbook*. Reading, MA: Addison-Wesley, 1981.

———. *Learning from Cooking Experiences*. Reading, MA: Addison-Wesley, 1981.

Anyone can cook with children and any child can cook. The recipes in this terrific book are shown in simple picture sequence form. They are easy to follow, nutritious, and drawn from different parts of the world.

16

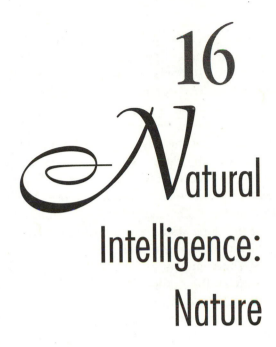

Natural Intelligence: Nature

[Children] find infinite appeal in soil and mud, in sand and water, in making colorful marks on paper; later they enjoy the discipline of wood, of stone and rock, of sound and light. It is the crust of the earth, in all its variations, which most attracts the child. In handling these things, the child's powers of concentration are exercised to the full.

ALICE YARDLEY
Young Children Thinking

Gardner's theory of multiple intelligences has given me a dynamic framework for supporting children's learning. What I enjoy most is that the theory is a living, growing body of practice. There are new wonderings to be had all the time.

A few years ago, I found myself teaching a grade three/four class for learners with behavioral and academic exceptionalities. Such jobs are never easy, and I relied on my teaching partner, a trained specialist in working with such learners. Over the year, I was reminded of the satisfaction of small accomplishments and learned to revise the day's plans at a moment's notice. By the end of May, I was more physically fatigued than I had ever been before.

Naturally, we had scheduled a three-day trip to an outdoor education center far out of the city at the beginning of June. The plans took shape early in the year when optimism and energy were high. I can remember watching the weather forecasts intently hoping for clear, sunny weather so we could be outside as much as possible. On the appointed day, we arrived and got our luggage into the cabins, ate lunch, and went outside for our first long walk. It began to rain. Hard.

We carried on anyway and hiked a muddy trail leading deep into the woods. There, mostly sheltered from the rain, we slowly became aware of the magic of the outdoors—the earthy smells, the sudden movement of wildlife in the trees, the insects, worms, and leaves at our feet. We were transported to another place altogether. A general sense of calm and good-natured camaraderie enveloped us.

The moment didn't last much beyond the boundary of the woods. As we left, one of the wiser of the children turned back and wistfully announced that he could have stayed in that quiet place forever. The others looked back and nodded in agreement.

Over the years, I've read about one person or another proposing that Gardner add this or that intelligence. When I have given workshops, participants have asked why the visual arts aren't an intelligence unto themselves, and so on. Gardner invites some of this, because he has stated that there may be more than his seven core intelligences. Now he has added an eighth: "Recently, I have enlarged my list to include an eighth form of intelligence: the apprehension of the natural world, as epitomized by skilled hunters or botanists" (1997, p. 36).

Any intelligence needs an environment in which to grow, but in this chapter, we come to one that is, in a very real sense, alive and responsive to our thoughts. I wonder if what took him so long to decide on this intelligence is the fact that places for expressing this intelligence are diminishing. Many children, even in rural areas, have fewer of these wild places to visit than they used to (Trimble 1996). Even in fairly urban settings where I grew up, I can remember finding little places along riverbanks or small creeks running down from fields. They were small, safe places for small, safe adventures. From such safe perches, one could imagine bigger adventures. Such places still exist, but now they aren't always safe for children to visit.

NATURE AS AN ENTRY POINT

Aside from viewing the "apprehension of the natural world" as a distinct intelligence, there is also a strong case to be made for using the natural world as an entry point to other subjects. Human history has been shaped and modified by geographic location, terrain, and climate. It is not an accident that so many early civilizations took hold where they did—near water, in mountain strongholds, along trade routes. Every era has been marked by plagues and medical breakthroughs, crop failures and bumper harvests.

Patterns in nature resonate with mathematical precision. Shells, leaves, and animals evidence symmetries that can be expressed in complex formulations. Over the last twenty years a whole branch of mathematics called *chaos theory* has arisen to account for the variations and seeming unpredictability of the natural world.

Literature is filled with stories of people at odds with the natural world, surviving the forces of nature, or studying its beauty and power. There is even a vein of science fiction running from Jules Verne (*20,000 Leagues Under the Sea*) to the present that imagines practical, detailed solutions for surviving in oceans or making Mars habitable for humans (*Red Mars* by Kim Stanley Robinson).

A Passion for Bugs

Actually, you probably don't want to know this, but many classrooms are full of live insects having a perfectly wonderful life cycle right underneath your nose. Into my partner Carol's morning kindergarten, smack in the middle of the city, came a serious five-year-old. Even passing through, it was hard not to notice that Jermaine seemed to like lying on the ground, staring intently. On one occasion, I watched him wriggle into an impossibly small corner and stay there, as silent as could be, for some time. As often as not, he would rise from these little expeditions with some kind of insect. Spiders of all kinds, shapes, and sizes dominated, but there were also centipedes and a host of insects that we weren't quite sure what to call. And this was *indoors*. Outdoors it was a similar story, though there needed to be strong direction not to strip off a layer of topsoil to get to "the bugs."

Such a passion inevitably influences the direction of a program. Carol made bug-collecting jars available and ordered large magnifiers. She acquired books about bugs for the class library. Insects became the hot topic for many of the children in Carol's class. But what is most interesting of all is that the passion for insects spilled over from the morning class into the afternoon class because of the bug-related material all over the classroom.

In a way, children's interest in insects needs little prompting and extends in many directions. Many superheroes are insect related or are drawn from images of the natural world (Spiderman, Batman). What is Halloween if not a time for spider webs and insect images? Some of the children's favorite folk stories tell of the exploits of Anansi the spider. One of the great trickster figures in folklore, he is a character many children identify with because of his small size. Bugs, the topic, goes off in as many directions as bugs, the real thing.

Multiple intelligence theory has certainly made me an advocate on behalf of children. I also wonder about the children you sometimes see in a field or near a garden, watching the ducks on a river or studying the patterns of a flower, who just seem "in their element" in natural surroundings. I am reminded of specific students of long ago, a boy from a village by the ocean, stuck in the big city, who would regularly skip school to go to the river and look for fish. He knew a great deal about fish, and his prized possession was a poster from a fish processing company that listed all kinds of fish. I remember a girl who always watered the plants in the classroom. It was assumed that she did this because it was a long-standing routine, but now I look back and wonder if we missed something.

In terms of classroom environment, I have always had plants and animals in the room. Taking care of a living thing is very rewarding all by itself. Gerbils are my favorite because they are neat, clean, and live a long time (almost three years and counting as I write). Best of all, they allow themselves to be held and would happily crawl up and in and around clothing, forcing children to be careful not to hurt them. They also need to be fed and their cage cleaned, both prized duties on the class duty roster.

I have also learned to run an aquarium. Fish are not warm and cuddly, but they are wonderful to watch as they glide and dart through the water and create a calm, quiet mood. Children are fascinated that some fish are so hard to find or that snail populations occasionally explode and take over

Figure 16a   One of Jermaine's many animal drawings.

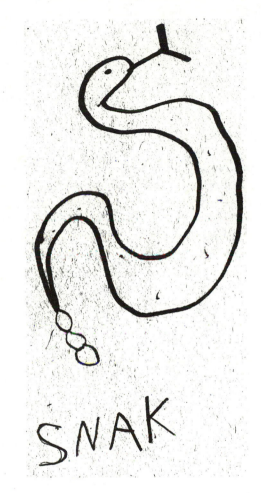

a tank. In one year, finding and counting the snails amid the plant life in the tank became a real "wheres Waldo?" search.

Building Natural Places

By looking forward, we find ourselves in new places. It is important to work with people who have certain passions and strong beliefs and to try to make room for these passions and beliefs. I have no particular aptitude for gardening, but I work with colleagues at my school, Lambton Park, who have a passion for carving out natural spaces in the city for children to experience. Over the last year, I have seen the schoolyard transformed into a welcoming space with a large, multi-tiered, sandbox, a small bridge attached to the sandbox, a pergola, and the beginnings of a garden. With some luck, in a few years there will be gardens everywhere.

As it is, our gardens include a vegetable patch. With the children, we fertilize the ground and plant tomatoes, lettuce, carrots, and onions. For city children to go out and pick vegetables to use in our hot lunch program connects their lives in a deep way with the natural world. The worms in our indoor composters turn the leftovers into fertilizer for our plants.

We also go out and plant bulbs we have picked out with the children. What better way to demonstrate the passage of time then to plant in the fall and see the colorful results in the spring? We also plant wildflowers with the children in various corners of our little yard. We have added large chunks of a tree trunk to provide a shady place for them.

We have also begun to attract birds by putting suction cup feeders on our windows. I can genuinely point out to the children that I too am just learning the best ways to feed the birds. We compare kinds of seeds, how fast the birds eat the seeds, and even the rate at which they eat from different feeders.

A marvelous sense of awe falls over the kindergarten as children watch the birds eating at these feeders. They learn to be quiet in the most attentive ways. In a world where many claim that children have short attention spans, it is a gentle reminder of the ways in which environment supports intelligence.

Leslie Moir and Elizabeth Cowling, two teachers at Lambton Park, wanted to use plants to build self-esteem: Learning to take care of a plant is like learning to take care of yourself. You both need good food, fresh air, sunlight, and people to take care of you.

Their studies were far ranging. Children asked plant questions, carried out science investigations, grew plants of all kinds, and cooked with herbs. However, the most interesting project began quietly as a plan to make an alphabet book about plants to be read to younger children. It was here that all their research on plants and their passion for plants came out. They included journal entries comparing reading to younger children to taking care of plants. They added fact upon fact. Challenged to find a plant or plant topic to go with each letter, they did.

Each page also needed an illustration. Here the work began to take on its own dazzling momentum as they created page after page of paintings.

Figure 16b   Reflection and nature seem to go hand in hand.

The detail and craft that went into each served as a reminder that painting, like writing, needs an authentic context and a real audience to succeed.

In his journal entry, Victor reflected that "Taking care of a reading buddy was like taking care of a plant." It was one of the first uses of a nature entry point I had seen.

Moments like this encourage us to continue.

Over the next couple of years the schoolyard will be transformed. There are good reasons to embark on a schoolyard naturalization project. Children spend at least eighteen hundred hours (257 days) of their school careers outside (Cheskey 1996). Learning cannot be conceived of as occurring only within four walls.

Recently, the entire school was invited to submit drawings, sketches, and other ideas what they might like to see in a schoolyard. Children and teachers watched videos and looked at photographs of other naturalized schoolyard spaces to start them off. So many of us have spent so long in urban settings, we can't imagine what a naturalized yard might be. The plans give consideration to some of the different types of spaces that have been shown to have a calming effect. These include large spaces with vistas, places with open water, and places to hide and crawl through (Cheskey 1994).

Different spaces, even outdoors, give the intelligences room to grow: large, open spaces for those who need to move; quiet contained spaces for those who need to reflect; meeting places for small groups, such as tree stumps with checkerboards and table spaces for books. We want to create places where children have the pride of knowing that they themselves are the owners and caretakers. Such children would truly start to see connections between themselves and their environment.

These discussions, in and of themselves, have begun to affect the direction of the dancing class. Children pore over nature magazines at reading times and announce bird sightings on the way to school in excited voices. Plants, ever-present, now attract more attention. When a large hyacinth in the corner bloomed, it caused much excitement.

But the most profound moment came in another kindergarten, where Margaret Shugg, the childcare coordinator, had just finished a presentation inviting students to think about what they wanted in a yard. One boy, who clearly had a passion for the subject and offered all sorts of observations, ran up to Margaret, gave her a long hug, and said, ''Thank you for coming to talk to me.''

ENDINGS

It has been a over twelve years since I first read Gardner's *Frames of Mind.* I've changed employers, careers, and cities. I've changed my mind about hundreds of things. I learn more every day when I walk into a classroom, open a book, or talk to a colleague. Through it all, the theory and the practice associated with multiple intelligences has stayed with me. Touching as it may be, I don't think children should have to come up to us and thank us for teaching in ways they understand. For me the theory of multiple intelligences is a practitioner's theory. It makes sense in the classroom. More important, the directions in which Gardner has taken it have continued to yield answers to some of my ongoing questions. It includes children, begins with their interests, fits with new technologies, and lets children see themselves as learners. If that's not enough, it is a living theory that sparks new stories and new ideas.

Thank you for coming to listen to me tell some of the stories of intelligence. I hope at least a few have taken you back, and caused you to reflect and wonder if . . .

RECOMMENDED READING

Picture Books

Cabral, L., and D. Diaz. *Anansi's Narrow Waist.* Glenview, IL: Scott, Foresman, 1993.

Kimmel, E. A., and J. Stevens. *Anansi and the Talking Melon.* New York: Holiday House, 1994.

McDermott, Gerald. *Anansi the Spider: A Tale from the Ashanti.* New York: Henry Holt, 1972.

> Anansi is very popular with children of all grades and levels. I think children identify with Anasi because he is so small, and surrounded by more powerful creatures, yet manages to outwit them. These are just three of the many Anansi stories. While none of these books includes any particular information about spiders, I have found that they do get children more interested in spiders.

Ray, M. L., and L. Stringer. *Mud.* New York: Harcourt Brace, 1996.

> This book tells of the coming of spring and mud, with all of it's sensory properties. The pictures show many close-ups of hands and feet squishing in mud, and the text is poetic. This is absolutely at the top of this year's kindergarten favorites.

Weisner, David. *June 29, 1999.* New York: Clarion Books, 1992.

> A humorous book about a science experiment. A girl launches seeds into the air. Days later, huge vegetables the size of houses start to appear. However, not all the vegetables falling from the sky are those the girl sent up, and she is left wondering about what happened to her plants. This book actually outlines the scientific method. It is one of kindergarten's favorite books (possibly because the vegetables turn out to come from an alien spaceship).

Reference Books

Cornell, Joseph. *Sharing the Joy of Nature: Nature Activities for All Ages.* Nevada City, CA: Dawn Publications, 1989.

> A well-outlined set of practices for getting children into nature and reflecting on what it means for them. Cornell calls his approach "flow learning" and I have found it to be a useful framework for exploring nature with children.

Nabahan, Gary Paul, and Stephen Trimble. *The Geography of Childhood: Why Children Need Wild Places.* Boston, MA: Beacon Press, 1994.

A very enjoyable collection of essays about children, nature, and learning. The tone is sometimes reflective, sometimes mournful over what we have lost. Above all, it is a passionate call to create more wild places for children. This particular book inspired me to bring more of the natural world to my urban children.

The Nomad Scientists. *Link Science: A Hands-on Approach to the Environment.* Markham, ON: Pembroke Publishers, 1990.

Another very practical, get-your-hands-dirty kind of book. Young children are quick to care about environmental issues, especially when they realize that they can make a difference.

References

Ackerman, D. 1990. *A Natural History of the Senses.* New York: Random House.

Affolter, F. 1987. *Perception, Interaction in Language: Interaction of Daily Living: The Root of Development.* Berlin, Heidelberg: Springer-Verlag.

Armstrong, T. 1994. *Multiple Intelligences in the Classroom.* Alexandria, VA: Association for Supervision and Curriculum Development.

Astington, J. 1993. *The Child's Discovery of Mind.* Cambridge, MA: Harvard University Press.

Atherly, S., and M. Halsey. 1995. *Math in the Bath (and Other Fun Places, Too!)* New York: Simon and Schuster Books for Young Readers.

Auer, M., and S. Klages. 1988. *Now, Now, Markus or I Need a Bird* [originally published in the Federal Republic of Germany under the title *Bimbo und sein Vogel.* Translated in 1990].

Baker, D., C. Semple, and T. Stead. 1990. *How Big Is the Moon?: Whole Maths in Action.* Portsmouth, NH: Heinemann.

Baron, J. B., and R. J. Sternberg, eds. 1987. *Teaching Thinking Skills: Theory and Practice.* New York: W. H. Freeman.

Barton, B., and D. Booth. 1990. *Stories in the Classroom: Storytelling, Reading Aloud and Roleplaying with Children.* Markham, ON: Pembroke Publishers.

Beesey, C., and L. Davie. 1994. *Maths Talk: Understanding and Using the Language of Mathematics.* South Melbourne: MacMillan Educational Australia.

Berman, M. 1990. *Coming to Our Senses: Body and Spirit in the Hidden History of the West.* Toronto: Bantam Books.

Bloom, B. 1956. *Taxonomy of Educational Objectives: The Classification of Educational Goals. Book 1: Cognitive Domain.* New York: Longman.

Bodrova, E., and D. Leong. 1996. *Tools of the Mind: The Vygotskian Approach to Early Childhood Education.* Toronto: Prentice Hall.

Bohm, D., and F. D. Peat. 1987. *Science, Order and Creativity.* Toronto: Bantam Books.

Booth, W. 1988. *The Company We Keep: An Ethics of Fiction.* Berkeley, CA: University of California Press.

Bosak, S. V. 1992. *Science Is . . . A Source Book of Fascinating Facts, Projects and Activities.* Toronto: Scholastic Canada/The Communication Project.

Brandt, R. 1987/1988. "On Assessment in the Arts: A Conversation with Howard Gardner." *Educational Leadership* 45: 30–34.

Brissenden, T. 1988. *Talking About Mathematics: Mathematical Discussions in Primary Classrooms.* Oxford: Basil Blackwell.

Brown, M. W. 1949. *The Important Book.* Illus. L. Weisgard. New York: Harper and Row.

Bruner, J. 1986. *Actual Minds, Possible Worlds.* Cambridge, MA: Harvard University Press.

———. 1990. *Acts of Meaning.* Cambridge, MA: Harvard University Press.

Bruner, J. and C. Feldman. 1990. "Metaphors of Consciousness and Cognition in the History of Psychology." In *Metaphors in the History of Psychology,* ed. D. E. Leary. New York: Cambridge University Press.

Bruner, J. and S. Weisser. 1991. "The Invention of Self: Autobiography and Its Forms." In *Literacy and Orality,* ed. D. Olson and N. Torrance, 129–148. Cambridge, MA: Cambridge University Press.

Burke, K., R. Fogarty, and S. Belgrad. 1994. *The Portfolio Connection.* Palatine, IL: IRI/Skylight Publishing.

Burston, P., and A. Graham. 1990. *The Funfair of Evil.* London: Walker Books.

Cabral, L., and D. Diaz. 1993. *Anansi's Narrow Waist.* Glenview, IL: Scott, Foresman.

Cambourne, B. 1988. *The Whole Story: Natural Learning and the Acquisition of Literacy in the Classroom.* Auckland, NZ: Ashton Scholastic.

Cassidy, D., and C. Lancaster. 1993. "The Grassroots Curriculum: A Dialogue Between Children and Teachers." *Young Children,* 48: pp. 47–51.

Cassidy, J. 1991. *Explorabook: A Kids' Science Museum in a Book.* Palo Alto, CA: Klutz Press.

———. 1994. *Earthsearch: A Kid's Geography Museum in a Book.* Palo Alto, CA: Klutz Press.

Chambers, A. 1985. *Booktalk: Occasional Writing on Literature and Children.* London: Bodley Head.

———. 1996. *Tell Me: Children, Reading, and Talk.* York, ME: Stenhouse Publishers; Markham, ON: Pembroke Publishers.

Cheskey, E. 1994. "Habitat Restoration." *FWTAO Newsletter, September/October.*

———. 1996. "How Schoolyards Influence Behavior: What Common Sense and Research Tell Us." *Green Teacher,* 47: 11–14.

Cole, B. 1987. *The Trouble with Dad.* London, UK: Collins Publishing Group.

Coles, R. 1986a. *The Moral Life of Children.* Boston: Atlantic Monthly Press.

———. 1986b. *The Political Life of Children.* Boston: Atlantic Monthly Press.

Cornell, J. 1989. *Sharing the Joy of Nature: Nature Activities for All Ages.* Nevada City, CA: Dawn Publications.

Costa, A. L. 1991. *The School as a Home for the Mind.* Palatine, IL: IRI/Skylight Publishing.

Csikszentmihalyi, M. 1990. *Flow: The Psychology of Optimal Experience.* New York: Harper and Row.

———. 1996. *Flow and the Psychology of Discovery and Invention.* New York: HarperCollins.

de Bono, E. 1973. *Lateral Thinking. Creativity Step by Step.* New York: Harper and Row.

Dewey, J. 1966. *Democracy and Education.* New York: Free Press. Originally published in 1916.

Donaldson, M. 1993. *Human Minds: An Exploration.* Toronto: Penguin Books.

Duchan, J. 1991. "Everyday Events: Their Role in Language Assessment and Intervention." In *Pragmatics of Language: Clinical Practice Issues,* ed. T. Gallagher. San Diego, CA: Singular Publishing Group.

Egan, K. 1986. *Teaching as Storytelling: An Alternative Approach to Teaching and Curriculum in the Elementary School.* London, ON: Althouse Press, Faculty of Education, University of Western Ontario.

———. 1988. *Primary Understanding: Education in Early Childhood.* New York: Routledge.

Elkind, D. 1981. *The Hurried Child.* Reading, MA: Addison-Wesley.

Engel, S. 1995. *The Stories Children Tell: Making Sense of the Narratives of Childhood.* New York: Freeman.

Feuerstein, R., with Y. Rand, M. Hoffman, and Ronald Miller. 1979. *The Dynamic Assessment of Retarded Performers: The Learning Potential Assessment Device, Theory, Instruments, and Techniques.* Baltimore, MD: University Park Press.

Flavell, J. H., F. L. Green, and E. R. Flavell. 1995. "Young Children's Knowledge About Thinking." *Monographs of the Society for Research in Child Development,* 60 (Serial No. 243, No. 1).

Gardner, H. 1980. *Artful Scribbles: The Significance of Children's Drawings.* New York: Basic Books.

———. 1981. *The Quest for Mind: Piaget, Levi-Strauss, and the Structuralist Movement,* 2d ed. Chicago: University of Chicago Press. Originally published in 1972.

———. 1982. *Art, Mind, and Brain: A Cognitive Approach to Creativity.* New York: Basic Books.

———. 1983. *Frames of Mind: The Theory of Multiple Intelligences.* New York: Basic Books.

———. 1989. *To Open Minds.* New York: Basic Books.

———. 1991. *The Unschooled Mind: How Children Think and How Schools Should Teach.* New York: Basic Books.

———. 1993a. *Creating Minds: An Anatomy of Creativity Seen Through the Lives of Freud, Einstein, Picasso, Stravinsky, Eliot, Graham, and Gandhi.* New York: Basic Books.

———. 1993b. *Multiple Intelligences: The Theory in Practice—A Reader.* New York: Basic Books.

———. 1994. *The Arts and Human Development.* New York: Basic Books. Originally published in 1973.

———. 1995. "Reflections on Multiple Intelligences." *Phi Delta Kappan, November,* 200–209.

———. 1996. "Probing More Deeply into the Theory of Multiple Intelligences." *Bulletin: The National Association of Secondary School Principals* 80, no. 583: 1–7.

———. 1997. *Extraordinary Minds: Portraits of Four Exceptional Individuals and an Examination of Our Own Extraordinariness.* New York: Basic Books.

Gardner, H., and L. Jaglom. 1982. "Cracking the Codes of Television: The Child as Anthropologist." In *Art, Mind, and Brain: A Cognitive Approach to Creativity,* H. Gardner. New York: Basic Books.

Gardner, H., and E. Laskin. 1995. *Leading Minds: An Anatomy of Leadership.* New York: Basic Books.

Gerstein, M. 1987. *The Mountains of Tibet.* New York: Harper and Row.

Giganti, P. 1992. *Each Orange Had 8 Slices: A Counting Book.* Illus. Donald Crews. New York: Greenwillow Books.

Goleman, D. 1995. *Emotional Intelligence: Why It Can Matter More Than IQ.* New York: Bantam Books.

Guilford, J. P. 1967. *The Structure of Intellect.* New York: McGraw-Hill.

Hardy, G. B. 1992. *A Mathematician's Apology.* Foreword by C. P. Snow. Cambridge: Cambridge University Press. Originally published in 1946.

Heath, S. B. 1983. *Ways with Words: Language, Life and Work in Communities and Classrooms.* New York: Cambridge University Press.

Hofstadter, D. 1979. *Gödel, Escher, Bach: An Eternal Golden Braid. A Metaphorical Fugue on Minds and Machines in the Spirit of Lewis Carroll.* New York: Basic Books.

Hunt, D. 1987. *Beginning with Ourselves: In Practice, Theory and Human Affairs.* Toronto: OISE Press.

Hyerle, D. 1996. *Visual Tools for Constructing Knowledge.* Alexandria, VA: Association for Supervision and Curriculum Development.

Johnson, A., and D. Soman. 1989. *Tell Me a Story, Mama.* New York: Orchard Books.

Johnson, M. 1987. *The Body in the Mind: The Bodily Basis of Meaning, Imagination, and Reason.* Chicago: University of Chicago Press.

———. 1993. *Moral Imagination: Implications of Cognitive Science for Ethics.* Chicago: Unversity of Chicago Press.

Johnson, T. D., and D. R. Louis. 1987. *Literacy Through Literature.* Richmond Hill, ON: Scholastic Canada.

Joyce, M. 1994. *First Steps in Teaching Creative Dance to Children.* 3rd. ed. Mountain View, CA: Mayfield.

Kimmel, E. A., and J. Stevens. 1994. *Anansi and the Talking Melon.* New York: Holiday House.

Krechevsky, M. 1994. *Project Spectrum: Preschool Assessment Handbook.* President and Fellows of Harvard College.

Kuhl, P. 1980. "Infant Speech Perception: Reviewing Data on Auditory Category Formation." In *Auditory Processing and Language: Clinical Research and Perspectives,* ed. C. Sloan and P. Levinson. New York: Grune and Stratton.

Lake, J. 1993. *Imagine: A Literature-Based Approach to Science.* Markham, ON: Pembroke Publishers.

Lakoff, G. 1987. *Women, Fire and Dangerous Things: What Categories Reveal About the Mind.* Chicago: University of Chicago Press.

Lakoff, G., and M. Johnson. 1980. *Metaphors We Live By.* Chicago: University of Chicago Press.

Leary, D. E., ed. 1990. *Metaphors in the History of Psychology.* New York: Cambridge University Press.

Lipman, M. 1991. *Thinking in Education.* Cambridge, MA: Cambridge University Press.

Lipman, M., A. M. Sharp, and F. S. Oscanyan. 1977. *Philosophy in the Classroom.* Upper Montclair, NJ: Institute for the Advancement of Philosophy for Children.

Luenn, N., and N. Waldman. 1994. *Nessa's Story.* New York: Macmillian.

Macauley, David. 1976. *Underground.* Boston: Houghton Mifflin.

Margulies, N. 1991. *Mapping Inner Space: Learning and Teaching Mind Mapping.* Tucson, AZ: Zephyr Press.

The Mathematical Association (U.K.) 1987. *Math Talk.*

Matthews, G. B. 1984. *Dialogues with Children.* Cambridge, MA: Harvard University Press.

———. 1994. *The Philosophy of Childhood.* Cambridge, MA: Harvard University Press.

McDermott, G. 1972. *Anansi the Spider: A Tale from the Ashanti.* New York: Henry Holt.

———. 1992. *Zomo the Rabbit: A Trickster Tale from West Africa.* New York: Harcourt Brace.

Meek, M. 1991. *On Being Literate.* London: Bodley Head Children's Books.

Metropolitan Toronto School Board. 1989. *The Child's World: Presenting Design and Technology.* Toronto: Metropolitan Toronto School Board.

———. 1997. *Responding to Media Violence: Starting Points for Classroom Practice.* Markham, ON: Pembroke Publishers.

Montgomery, R. A. 1981. *The Haunted House.* Toronto: Bantam Books.

Moore, R., ed. 1994. *Aesthetics for Young People.* Reprinted from *Journal of Aesthetic Education,* 28. Champaign, IL: University of Illinois.

Morgan, N., and J. Saxton. 1994. *Asking Better Questions: Models, Techniques and Classroom Activities for Engaging Students in Learning.* Markham, ON: Pembroke Publishers.

Myers, W. D., and A. Bryan. 1995. *The Story of Three Kingdoms.* New York: HarperCollins.

Nabahan, G. P., and S. Trimble. 1994. *The Geography of Childhood: Why Children Need Wild Places.* Boston, MA: Beacon Press.

Nelson, K., ed. 1989. *Narratives from the Crib.* Cambridge, MA: Harvard University Press.

The Nomad Scientists. 1990. *Link Science: A Hands-on Approach to the Environment.* Markham, ON: Pembroke Publishers.

O'Neill, M. 1961. *Hailstones and Halibut Bones.* Illus. J. Wallner. Toronto: Doubleday.

Olson, D. R. 1991. "Literacy as Metalinguistic Activity." In *Literacy and Orality,* ed. D. Olson and N. Torrance. Cambridge, MA: Cambridge University Press.

Ortony, A., ed. 1993. *Metaphor and Thought,* 2d ed. Cambridge, MA: Cambridge University Press.

Ostrow, J. 1995. *A Room with a Different View: First Through Third Graders Build Community and Create Curriculum.* York, ME: Stenhouse Publishers; Markham, ON: Pembroke Publishers.

Packard, E. 1988. *America: Why Is There an Eye on the Pyramid on the One Dollar Bill?* Toronto: McGraw Hill.

Paley, V. G. 1988. *Bad Guys Don't Have Birthdays: Fantasy Play at Four.* Chicago: University of Chicago Press.

———. 1990. *The Boy Who Would Be a Helicopter: The Uses of Storytelling in the Classroom.* Cambridge, MA: Harvard University Press.

———. 1992. *You Can't Say You Can't Play.* Cambridge, MA: Harvard University Press.

Paterson, Katherine. 1989. *The Spying Heart: More Thoughts on Reading and Writing Books for Children.* Toronto: Fitzhenry and Whiteside.

Pehrsson, R., and H. A. Robinson. 1985. *The Semantic Organizer Approach to Reading and Writing Instruction.* Rockville, MD: Aspen Publishers.

Pickering, J., and S. Attridge. 1990. "Viewpoints: Metaphors and Monsters—Children's Storytelling." *Research in the Teaching of English,* 24: 415–440.

Pimm, D. 1987. *Speaking Mathematically: Communication in Mathematics Classrooms.* London: Routledge and Kegan Paul.

Polkinghorne, D. E. 1988. *Narrative Knowing and the Human Sciences.* Albany, NY: State University of New York Press.

Pressley, M., K. Harris, and J. Guthrie. 1992. *Promoting Academic Competence and Literacy: Cognitive Research and Instructional Innovation.* New York: Academic.

Pribram, K. 1990. "From Metaphors to Models: The Use of Analogy in Neuropsychology." In *Metaphors in the History of Psychology,* ed. D. E. Leary. New York: Cambridge University Press.

Ray, M. L., and L. Stringer. 1996. *Mud.* New York: Harcourt Brace.

Reid, B., and R. Bringhurst. 1984. *The Raven Steals the Light.* Vancouver, Toronto, Seattle: Douglas and McIntyre, University of Washington Press.

Rieber, R. W., and A. S. Carton, eds. 1987. *The Collected Works of L. S. Vygotsky. Vol. 1. Problems of General Psychology.* New York: Plenum Press.

———. 1993. *The Collected Works of L. S. Vygotsky. Vol. 2. The Fundamentals of Defectology.* New York: Plenum Press.

Ross, M. 1984. *The Aesthetic Impulse.* Oxford: Pergamon Press.

Salomon, G. 1997. "Of Mind and Media: How Culture's Symbolic Forms Affect Learning and Thinking." *Phi Delta Kappan,* 78: 375–380.

Salomon, G., and H. Gardner. 1983. "The Computer as Educator: Lessons from Television Research." *ERIC Report.* Springfield, VA: U.S. Department of Education.

Schön, D. 1987. *Educating the Reflective Practitioner.* San Francisco: Jossey-Bass.

Schwartz, D. M., and S. Kellogg. 1985. *How Much Is a Million?* New York: William Morrow.

Scieszka, J., and L. Smith. 1995. *Math Curse.* New York: Penguin Books.

Seuss, Dr. 1975. *Oh the Thinks You Can Think.* New York: Random House Beginner Books.

———. 1996. *My Many Colored Days.* Illus. Steve Johnson and Lou Fancher. New York: Random House.

Smith, D. 1996. "Choose Your Own Writing." *Reading Teacher,* 49: p. 420.

Sternberg, R. J. 1985. *Beyond IQ: A Triarchic Theory of Human Intelligence.* Cambridge, MA: Cambridge University Press.

———. 1988. *The Triarchic Mind: A New Theory of Human Intelligence.* New York: Viking Penguin.

———. 1996. *Successful Intelligence: How Practical and Creative Intelligence Determines Success in Life.* New York: Simon and Schuster.

Strupp, P. 1994. *You Call the Play, Baseball: Catcher in Command.* Toronto: Bantam Books.

Tierney, R., M. Carter, and L. Desai. 1991. *Portfolio Assessment in the Reading-Writing Classroom.* Norwood, MA: Christopher Gordon.

Trimble, S. 1996. "A Land of One's Own." In *Geography of Childhood,* G. Nahaban and S. Trimble. Boston: Beacon Press.

Turkle, S. 1984. *The Second Self: Computers and the Human Spirit.* New York: Simon and Schuster.

———. 1995. *Life on the Screen: Identity in the Age of the Internet.* New York: Simon and Schuster.

Varela, F. J., E. Thompson, and E. Rosch. 1991. *The Embodied Mind: Cognitive Science and Human Experience.* Cambridge, MA: MIT Press.

Veitch, B., and T. Harms. 1981a. *Cook and Learn: A Child's Cookbook.* Reading, MA: Addison-Wesley.

———. 1981b. *Learning from Cooking Experiences.* Reading, MA: Addison-Wesley.

Viorst, J. 1971. *The Tenth Good Thing About Barney.* Illus. Erik Blegvad. New York: Collier Macmillan.

Vygotsky, L. S. 1962. *Thought and Language.* Cambridge, MA: MIT Press.

———. 1978. *Mind in Society: The Development of Higher Psychological Processes,* ed. M. Cole, V. John-Steiner, S. Scribner, F. Souberman. Cambridge, MA: Harvard University Press.

Wallach, G. P., and L. Miller. 1988. *Language Intervention and Academic Success.* Boston: Little, Brown.

Walters, J., and H. Gardner. 1984. "The Crystallizing Experience: Discovering an Intellectual Gift." *ERIC Report.* Springfield, VA: U.S. Department of Education.

Wasserman, S. 1990. *Serious Players in the Primary Classroom.* New York: Teachers College Press.

Wasserman, S., and J. W. G. Ivany. 1988. *Teaching Elementary Science: Who's Afraid of Spiders.* Toronto: Harper and Row.

Weisner, D. 1992. *June 29, 1999.* New York: Clarion Books.

Wellman, H. 1990. *The Child's Theory of Mind.* Cambridge, MA: MIT Press.

Wells, G. 1986. *The Meaning Makers: Children Learning Language and Using Language to Learn.* Portsmouth, NH: Heinemann.

Wells, G., and G. L. Chang-Wells. 1992. *Constructing Knowledge Together: Classrooms as Centers of Inquiry and Literacy.* Portsmouth, NH: Heinemann.

———. 1994. *Changing Schools from Within: Creating Communities of Inquiry.* Toronto: OISE Press.

Westby, C. E. 1985. "Learning to Talk—Talking to Learn: Oral-Literate Language Differences." In *Communication Skills and Classroom Success: Therapy Methodologies for Language-Learning Disabled Students,* ed. C. S. Simon. San Diego, CA: College-Hill Press.

———. 1988. "Children's Play: Reflections of Social Competence." In *Seminars in Speech and Language: Preschool Language Evaluation,* ed. E. Teas-Hester. Vol. 9: 1–15.

Whitmore, K., and C. Crowell. 1994. *Inventing a Classroom: Life in a Bilingual, Whole Language Learning Community.* York, ME: Stenhouse Publishers.

Wilkinson, J. A. 1993. *The Symbolic Dramatic Play—Literacy Connection: Whole Brain, Whole Body, Whole Learning.* Needham Heights, MA: Ginn Press.

Williams, H. 1991. *Stories in Art.* Brookfield, CT. Milbrook Press.

Williams, K. L. 1990. *Galimoto.* Illus. Catherine Stock. New York: Lothrop, Lee and Sheppard Books.

Winner, E. 1988. *The Point of Words: Children's Understanding of Metaphor and Irony.* Cambridge, MA: Harvard University Press.

Winner, E., and H. Gardner. 1993. "Metaphor and Irony: Two Levels of Understanding." In *Metaphor and Thought,* ed. A. Ortony. Cambridge, MA: Cambridge University Press.

Witherell, C., and N. Noddings, eds. 1991. *Stories Lives Tell—Narrative and Dialogue in Education.* New York: Teachers College Press; Portsmouth, NH: Heinemann.

Wolf, D. P. 1989. "Artistic Learning as Conversation." In *Children and the Arts.,* ed. D. Hargreaves. Bristol, PA: Open University Press.

Wood, D. 1988. *How Children Think and Learn.* Cambridge, MA: Basil Blackwell.

Wynne-Jones, T., and I. Wallad. 1988. *Architect of the Moon.* Toronto: Douglas and McIntyre.

Yardley, A. 1988a. *Exploration and Language.* Toronto: Rubicon Publishing.

———. 1988b. *Reaching Out.* Toronto: Rubicon Publishing.

———. 1988c. *Senses and Sensitivity.* Toronto: Rubicon Publishing.

———. 1989a. *Structure in Early Learning.* Toronto: Rubicon Publishing.

———. 1989b. *Young Children Thinking.* Toronto: Rubicon Publishing.

Yenawine, P. 1991a. *Lines.* The Museum of Modern Art. New York: Delacorte Press.

———. 1991b. *Stories.* The Museum of Modern Art. New York: Delacorte Press.

———. 1991c. *Shapes.* The Museum of Modern Art. New York: Delacorte Press.

Index